LANGUAGE AND LITERACY SERIES

Dorothy S. Strickland and Celia Genishi, SERIES EDITORS

ADVISORY BOARD: RICHARD ALLINGTON, DONNA ALVERMANN, KATHRYN AU,
EDWARD CHITTENDON, BERNICE CULLINAN, COLETTE DAIUTE,
ANNE HAAS DYSON, CAROLE EDELSKY, JANET EMIG,
SHIRLEY BRICE HEATH, CONNIE JUEL, SUSAN LYTLE

(Continued)

Critical Encounters in High School English

TEACHING LITERARY THEORY TO ADOLESCENTS

Deborah Appleman

FOREWORD BY ARTHUR N. APPLEBEE

Teachers College
Columbia University
New York and London

National Council of
Teachers of English
Urbana, Illinois

Published simultaneously by Teachers College Press, 1234 Amsterdam Avenue, New York, NY 10027 and the National Council of Teachers of English

Library of Congress Cataloging-in-Publication Data

Appleman, Deborah.
    Critical encounters in high school English : teaching literary theory to adolescents / Deborah Appleman ; foreword by Arthur N. Applebee.
      p.   cm.—(Language and literacy series)
    Includes bibliographical references and index.
    ISBN 0-8077-3974-X—ISBN 0-8077-3975-8
      1. English literature—Study and teaching (Secondary) 2. Literature—History and criticism—Theory, etc.—Study and teaching (Secondary) 3. American literature—Study and teaching (Secondary) 4. Literature—Study and teaching (Secondary) I. Title. II. Language and literacy series (New York, N.Y.)

PR33 .A66   2000
820'.71'273—dc21

                                         00-044338

ISBN 0-8077-3974-X (paper)
ISBN 0-8077-3975-8 (cloth)

NCTE Stock No. 30275

Printed on acid-free paper

Manufactured in the United States of America

07 06 05 04   8 7 6 5 4

For my parents, who encouraged my dreams
For John, who helped them come true

Contents

Foreword

DOES LITERARY THEORY have any use for anyone outside of graduate seminars in English? In this book Deborah Appleman argues boldly that it does. In fact, she demonstrates how an introduction to a variety of competing contemporary theories can enrich and enliven the high school literature lesson.

How difficult is literary theory? In university departments of English it usually is treated as something very difficult indeed—representing the cutting edge of current scholarship, where ambitious professors and their graduate students make, or break, their reputations. The debates are often rancorous, and the distance between them and anything a more general public might find relevant is often great. The gap is so large that many columnists have made a tradition of filling the slow week between Christmas and New Years by ridiculing the session titles at the annual meeting of the Modern Language Association, where debates about critical theory get played out in a semipublic forum each December.

In part because literary theory is seen as both difficult and irrelevant, very little of it is apparent in most American secondary schools. The key word here, of course, is "apparent," for the schools are filled with activities that have their origins in one or another literary theory. As new generations of teachers have emerged from college and university, they have brought the theoretical approaches of their college teachers with them. Thus, at various times new theoretical approaches to literature have meant an emphasis on philology, on literary history, on the preservation of culture through the Great Books, on moral values, on the historical and sociological context, and on New Critical close reading. In the high school curriculum, each new approach usually has been added on to previous activities rather than completely replacing them. The result often has been a hodgepodge of activities, most with legitimate although unarticulated roots in past theories and bearing no clear relationship to one another or to helping students clarify their understandings of the works they read.

In the present book, Deborah Appleman shows us that literary theory is neither irrelevant nor too difficult for classroom use, and indeed can be a good starting point in untangling the bits and pieces out of which current practice is constructed. Moving beyond the debates that sometimes have polarized graduate English departments, Appleman invites students to appropriate the tools of literary theory and to use them to guide their own readings and analyses. As her students try out the multiple perspectives of feminist criticism, reader response, Marxist criticism, and deconstruction, they gain a deeper understanding of the texts they are reading. Rather than one right way to approach a text, students come to understand that there are many ways, sometimes complementary and sometimes competing, in which a text can be construed.

Deborah Appleman's work is especially appealing to me because it nicely complements a variety of other things in which I have been involved. For some dozen years now, researchers at the Center on English Learning and Achievement have been working to develop better-grounded approaches to the teaching of English. On the one hand, Center research has documented the problems inherent in current practice, and on the other, it has sought to offer solutions that are grounded in our best understandings of effective teaching and learning. As one teacher put it in a Center-sponsored study (Applebee, 1993), current literary theories "are far removed from those of us who work the front lines!"(p. 122). The teacher's comment was (and still is) a fair one, in that only a few of the participants in the debates about literary theory have given much thought to what their theories might mean for how literature might be taught. But this is in fact the task that Appleman has taken on: She gives us detailed, classroom-based examples of how currently influential literary theory can enrich greatly the literature classroom for all students. By introducing students to the tools that competing theories provide, she helps them learn to take a critical stance toward the texts they read and to understand why and how a single text can yield multiple interpretations. Rather than being indoctrinated into one point of view, students in Appleman's classrooms develop the multiple perspectives that other research at the Center has shown to be essential in effective literature teaching and learning . As Judith Langer (1995) has put it in summarizing another body of Center research, such an approach provides a frame

> to help students and teachers use what they know better and more effectively—to voice their own ideas, to hear others in ways that push their own thinking, to be sensitive to viewpoints not necessarily their own, to think deeply and communicate clearly. . . . Such an approach will give them power—power of voice, control of their growing ideas, and the sense of a self that comes from participating in a group of peers who do not always share the same insights or interpretations but who respect one another enough to gain richness from diversity. (p. 144)

This is an appealing vision of what our classrooms can do, and Appleman's book will help get us there.

Arthur N. Applebee
Center on English Learning and Achievement
State University of New York at Albany

REFERENCES

Applebee, A. N. (1993). *Literature in the secondary school: Studies of curriculum and instruction in the United States.* Urbana, IL: National Council of Teachers of English.

Langer, J. A. (1995). *Envisioning literature: Literary understanding and literature instruction.* New York: Teachers College Press.

Preface

I'M STUBBORN. Ask my friends. When they say it can't be done, I feel like I have to try.

As a former high school English teacher who now teaches future teachers at a liberal arts college, I found myself in the center of a divide about contemporary literary theory. On one side of that divide were my high school teacher friends, most of whom initially found my interest in contemporary theory to be somewhat suspicious, a sure sign that my high school teaching self was fading into those impractical ivied halls. They were even more doubtful of my claims that it might be fun and profitable to try to integrate theory into their literature classes.

On the other side of the theory chasm were my college and university colleagues, literature and literacy education professors from a variety of institutions who, on one hand, bemoaned the lack of literary knowledge with which secondary students came to college and, on the other hand, deeply doubted that contemporary literary theory was within the intellectual grasp of most high school students. This book is the result of my attempt to bridge that gap.

For the past 5 years, I have spent a good deal of time in both urban and suburban schools, working closely with classroom teachers to develop ways to integrate literary theory into high school English. All of the activities found in the appendix actually have been used by me and other classroom teachers across the country with real high school students, deliciously varied in their abilities, lives, and perspectives.

I hope that the approaches described in this book will help teachers enrich their literature instruction by using contemporary literary theories. I hope that these approaches to reading literature will help students learn to read from a multiplicity of perspectives and, most of all, will encourage young people to develop the intellectual flexibility they need to read not only literary texts but the cultural texts that surround and often confuse them.

I am buoyed by the good will and support of many friends and col-

leagues who made the writing of this book possible. To my colleagues at Carleton College, especially John Ramsay, Elizabeth Ciner, Robert Tisdale, Frank Morral, Susan Jaret McKinstry, and my dear friends Clare Rossini and Joseph Byrne. You each know what you've done for me. Thank you. This book and my life in general would not be in the presentable shape they are without the able assistance of Lois Messal, assistant extraordinaire.

I also owe a debt of gratitude to Susan Hynds, an amazing source of love, laughter, and lessons for more than a decade; Michael Smith, for the title and much, much more; Mary Beth Hines, fellow traveler on the road of theory and an unwavering source of support; James Marshall, a central room in my "house of thought" and a cherished friend; two anonymous reviewers for Teachers College Press for their generous and helpful comments; Carol Chambers Collins of Teachers College Press for her steadfast support, confidence, and gentle strength; Norma Sciarra for her bibliographic assistance; and Rick Beach for helping to send me on my way.

Special thanks are due to Barbara Allen, "book buddy and kindred spirit," whose generosity and wisdom are infinite; the best friend and teacher I know, Martha Cosgrove, whose masterful teaching and loving friendship represent the single most important factor that made this book possible; and finally the memory of the late James Mackey—advisor, mentor, and friend— who taught me how to live a life where the twin passions of teaching and writing can coexist.

Introduction

Often literary theories change our views of a work of literature by proposing new distinctions or new categories for looking at the work. This is a bit like putting on a new set of glasses: suddenly you see things more clearly.

—Stephen Bonnycastle, *In Search of Authority*

IT IS THE CLASS PERIOD right after lunch. The students tumble in, distracted by their school's recent success in the state football tournament. The fluorescent light of the classroom is darker than usual; a threatening sky may bring the first blast of a long Minnesota winter. It is a smallish class, around 20 students, and the atmosphere seems comfortable, almost intimate.

The students have been reading Ibsen's *A Doll's House*. Jessie, a confident and creative student teacher, is anxious to put to use some of the contemporary literary theory that made her college English courses so interesting. She thought she might incorporate feminist literary theory to highlight the role of women in Ibsen's portrayal of nineteenth-century Norwegian society. She thought that feminist literary theory might help her students really see Nora's plight as she struggles to make meaning of her drab and bounded life, a life that wars with her imagination and ambition.

It hasn't been easy. The students haven't been at all captivated by the hand-me-down theory articles that Jessie pulled from her college notebooks. The students have never even heard the term "literary theory" before, even though their regular classroom teacher had clearly employed both New Critical and reader-response techniques. The students had even studied a variety of archetypes. But this—this *theory*—seemed new and strange. Worse, to some of the students it seemed artificial and contrived, a "teacher game" not unlike those transparent symbol hunts or fishing for themes, designed to make reading literature even more complicated than it already was. It seemed like a fancy tool with no instructions. Some of the male students in particular

were irritated by what they considered to be an unnatural forcing of feminist issues onto a difficult and burdensome text.

Announced as a special visitor from the neighboring college, I come armed with pink handouts, some cryptic notes on feminist literary theory, and a pair of RayBan sunglasses. The lenses of the glasses have been specially ground for driving. I pass the sunglasses around, ask students to look through them and, when all have tried them on, ask them to comment on what they noticed.

"The reds stand out; look at Katie's sweater." Katie blushes and someone cries, "Look at Katie's face!" "The greens are way green," says someone else. "Do the glasses turn colors that aren't green or red into green or red?" I ask. "No," someone replies. "They just seem to bring out what's already there. Bring it out, so you won't miss it." After I tell them what the glasses are for, someone volunteers, "I get it—red and green, stop and go. The glasses bring out what's there 'cause you can't afford *not* to see it."

I shuffle the handouts on literary theory and tell the students that what the sunglasses did for the green and red, literary theory does for the texts we read. It provides lenses designed to bring out what is already there but what we often miss with unaided vision. Like the sunglasses, contemporary theories highlight particular features of what lies in our line of vision. If used properly, they do not create colors that weren't there in the first place; they only bring them into sharper relief. And, like the sunglasses, they have purpose outside the classroom. There are things we can't afford *not* to see.

I fold together the bows of my RayBans and ask the students to open the pages of their Ibsen. "There's a critical lens I'd like you to peer through," I say. "Let's see what we encounter."

The Case for Critical Theory in the Classroom

Critical lenses are about looking into elements of the world in different ways, thinking about things from different perspectives. This will never be a bad thing, no matter what the lenses are used to view. Seeing many different sides of stories only benefits everyone, everything.

—Mark, Grade 11

To read the world is to notice, to understand, and to interpret. The world around us needs all the lenses, and to use them is to respond to the world itself.

—Jenny, Grade 12

[L]iterary theory can handle Bob Dylan just as well as John Milton.
—Terry Eagleton, *Literary Theory*

WE LIVE IN DANGEROUS and complicated times and no one is more aware of it than our teenagers. How do we even begin to make our way through such a difficult and complicated world? As we begin our apprehensive march into the twenty-first century, we educators find ourselves reconsidering how our schools might help young people lead productive and satisfying lives. How do we help them negotiate these treacherous times? What can we do to make things better for them, to make schools safer and more productive places to grow and to learn?

Research on literacy practices, child and adolescent development, and school reform initiatives has tried to address these questions by focusing on urgent issues such as class size, qualifications of teachers, the sociocultural contexts of schooling, the out-of-school lives and challenges of children, and the requirements to make classrooms safe spaces. In the face of today's turbulence and the seemingly urgent need for pragmatic education, it seems almost ludicrous to suggest that the study of literary theory could have any relevance to the education of young people.

Literary theory? When guns go off in school hallways and on playgrounds? When 14-year-old children become mothers and fathers? When adolescents kill each other and themselves with frightening frequency? When many children and grownups don't read anything at all, let alone read with theory? Many people consider literary theory (if they consider it at all) as arcane and esoteric. It's dismissed as a sort of intellectual parlor game played by MLA types whose conference paper topics are the annual object of ridicule by the *New York Times*. As Terry Eagleton (1983) put it, "There are some who complain that literary theory is impossibly esoteric—who suspect it as an arcane elitist enclave somewhat akin to nuclear physics" (p. vii). What could poststructuralism, new historicism, deconstruction, Marxism, and feminist literary theory possibly have to do with the average adolescent, just struggling to grow up, stay alive, get through school, and make the most of things? Why, it sounds almost like suggesting that passengers taste truffles as the Titanic sinks. It sounds as if I'm promoting a sort of theoretical fiddling while the Rome of our sacred vision of successful public education burns.

Teachers, too, may not be convinced of the relevance of contemporary literary theory. High school literature teachers often feel distant and detached from recent developments in literary theory. Literature teachers find it difficult to see, at least initially, how contemporary literary theory can inform their daily practice. They are already overwhelmed as they juggle curricular concerns as well as the competing literacy skills and needs of their increasingly diverse student body. Students and teachers alike find it hard to believe that something as abstract and "impractical" as literary theory could be relevant to their lives, both in and out of the classroom. Nothing, however, could be further from the truth.

This book challenges current theoretical and pedagogical paradigms of the teaching of literature by incorporating the teaching of literary theory into high school literature classes. The guiding assumption of the book is that the direct teaching of literary theory in secondary English classes will better prepare adolescent readers to respond reflectively and analytically to literary texts, both "canonical" and multicultural. The book argues that contemporary literary theory provides a useful way for all students to read and interpret not only literary texts but their lives—both in and out of school. In its own way, reading with theory is a radical educational reform!

Like the RayBans in the introduction, literary theories provide lenses that can sharpen one's vision and provide alternative ways of seeing. Literary theories augment our sometimes failing sight. They bring into relief things we fail to notice. Literary theories recontextualize the familiar and comfortable, making us reappraise it. They make the strange seem oddly familiar. As we view the dynamic world around us, literary theories can become critical lenses to guide, inform, and instruct us.

Critical lenses provide students with a way of reading their world; the lenses provide a way of "seeing" differently and analytically that can help them read the culture of school as well as popular culture. Learning to inhabit multiple ways of knowing also can help them learn to adapt to the intellectual perspectives and learning styles required by other disciplines. When taught explicitly, literary theory can provide a repertoire of critical lenses through which to view literary texts as well as the multiple contexts at play when students read texts—contexts of culture, curriculum, classroom, personal experience, prior knowledge, and politics. Students can see what factors have shaped their own world view and what assumptions they make as they evaluate the perspectives of others, whether a character from a text, an author or literary movement, an MTV video, a shampoo commercial, peer pressure, or the school system in which they find themselves. As Bonnycastle (1996) points out, studying theory

> means you can take your own part in the struggles for power between different ideologies. It helps you to discover elements of your own ideology, and understand why you hold certain values unconsciously. It means no authority can impose a truth on you in a dogmatic way—and if some authority does try, you can challenge that truth in a powerful way, by asking what ideology it is based on. . . . Theory is subversive because it puts authority in question. (p. 34)

Perhaps even more important, these multiple ways of seeing have become vital skills in our increasingly diverse classrooms as we explore the differences between and among us, what separates us and what binds us together. As Maxine Greene (1993) has eloquently argued, "Learning to look through multiple perspectives, young people may be helped to build bridges among themselves; attending to a range of human stories, they may be provoked to heal and to transform" (p. 16). Attending to multiplicity, to the diversity that has come to characterize our interpretive communities, has caused some scholars to reconsider the role that literary theory may play as we acknowledge our need to learn to read across and between cultures (Rogers & Soter, 1997). As Laura Desai (1997) points out, "Literary theory reminds us that we do not live in isolation nor do we read and interpret in isolation. We understand what we read through some combination of ourselves as readers and the text with which we interact, but this is never free of the multiple contexts that frame us" (p. 169). Desai further argues that literary theory can provide for young people the tools necessary for interpreting culture as well. "Literary theory allows us to recognize our own reactions by providing the contexts we need to understand them. In this complex world, cultural forces are clearly at play in the lives of young people." But young people will remain powerless over these forces unless they can recognize

them: "How can we judge culture's impact if we cannot define what it is that is influencing our reactions?" (p. 170). Literary theory provides the interpretive tools young people need to recognize and "read" those cultural forces.

BACKGROUND, OR A BRIEF THEORETICAL HISTORY

Literary theory clearly has informed and in many ways shaped pedagogical practice, but in a monolithic, almost corrective way. That is, a single theoretical vision tends to dominate the teaching of literature until it is replaced by another. For example, literary study in high schools initially was dominated by Matthew Arnold's view of literary study as "cultural transmissiveness," a view in which texts are presented to young readers as cultural treasures to be honored unquestioningly. The influence of the New Critical perspective, most notably the work of I. A. Richards and the anthologies of Brooks and Warren, took hold of the secondary English classroom in the 1930s and is still felt today. In this model, the teacher becomes the primary explicator of the meaning of the text, correcting wrong or ill-conceived responses. This model gave rise to the primacy of the text in the literature classroom and to the authority of teachers as the definitive determiners of literary meaning.

Over the past 2 decades, reader-response theory has found its way into secondary classrooms. A reader-response approach to the teaching of literature allows students to employ a variety of interpretive strategies and encourages students to bring their personal experience to the text. Although the emphasis of this critical approach focuses on the reader rather than the teacher or text as the source of literary meaning, the problem of a single dominant theoretical perspective remains. In many high school classrooms, reader response has become the current orthodoxy of English education (Marshall, 1991). Students may be able to derive a plurality of interpretations using the reader-response approach, but they are still not presented with multiple critical approaches, which would enable them to choose and construct their own readings from a variety of theoretical perspectives rather than simply the perspective of personal response.

Broadly stated, teachers often feel torn between either presenting literary texts as cultural artifacts—literary masterpieces whose authoritative meaning is to be mastered by neophyte students—or relying heavily on students' personal experience through a reader-response approach. This tension between two theoretical traditions is noted by Applebee (1993) when he writes, "Though teachers make a practical compromise with these two traditions by drawing on both, the resulting eclecticism produces tensions and inconsistencies within the classroom rather than a coherent and integrated approach to the teaching and learning of literature" (p. 202). While the re-

sulting compromise in instruction may be due to competing theoretical approaches, teaching literature remains largely atheoretical, both for secondary teachers and for their students. Rarely do high school teachers make their theoretical approaches explicit by naming them to their students. And even more rarely have multiple critical approaches been explicitly taught.

THE CHANGING TIMES

As we begin a second century of teaching literature, it is time we examine these enduring characteristics of literature instruction, asking which are appropriate and essential and which have continued because they have remained unexamined.
> —Arthur N. Applebee, *Literature in the Secondary School*

In the past few decades, the relatively stable (some might even say staid) and predictable practice of teaching literature has undergone changes from a myriad of directions. At the prompting of scholars, practitioners, and, perhaps most important, the changing nature of our students, we have considered and reconsidered the texts, contexts, and pedagogical approaches that constitute the teaching of literature. Our canons are loose, our pedagogy is shifting, and our profession seems to be challenging every assumption we have made about the teaching of literature since 1920. For example, we have reconsidered the relationship of texts to readers, of readers and teachers to authors, of texts to theories, and, of course, of teachers to their students. Multicultural literature has largely been embraced by many teachers, but the complexity of teaching diverse works to diverse and nondiverse classes is just beginning to be confronted.

Our profession is challenging its assumptions about our literary heritage, our students, and even who is included in the pronoun *our*. This reflection demands that as we challenge the hegemony of the sort of "cultural literacy" proposed by Alan Bloom or E. D. Hirsch, we also challenge the notion of a single theory, perspective, or "truth" about what literature we read together and how we teach it. As Slevin and Young (1995) put it:

If texts no longer organize the curriculum, then what does? If the professor is no longer the privileged agent of education then who is? . . . These pressing questions . . . contemplate the end of coverage as a model, the end of the canon as an agreed-upon certainty, the end of the professor as the agent of learning, and the end of the classroom as a place where education is delivered. These "ends" have been much contemplated, indeed. But what arises in their place? (pp. ix–x)

THE CALL FOR THEORY

In the past decade or so, critical theory has played an increasingly important role in professional conversations among college literature professors and has become more visible in college literature classrooms as part of what it means to study literature. Slevin and Young (1995) regard theory as the site of some of our most profound professional re-examinations as we reconceptualize what it means to teach literature: "The new directions in literary theory and criticism that mark the last two decades can be seen as responses to these very concerns, reexamining the assumptions that underlie literary study" (pp. ix–x).

Similarly, Bonnycastle (1996) writes:

> Literary theory raises those issues which are often left submerged beneath the mass of information contained in the course, and it also asks questions about how the institution of great literature works. . . . What makes a "great work" great? Who makes the decisions about what will be taught? Why are authors grouped into certain historical periods? The answers to fundamental questions like these are often unarticulated assumptions on the part of both the professor and the students. . . . Literary theory is at its best when it helps us realize what we are really doing when we study literature. (p. 20)

In 1983, Terry Eagleton wrote, "Not much of this theoretical revolution has yet spread beyond a circle of specialists and enthusiasts: it still has to make its full impact on the student of literature and the general reader" (p. vii). More than a decade later, the presence of literary theory was more clearly (some might argue, oppressively) present in the college literature classroom, yet these developments in theory and the reconsiderations of curriculum that they generated had not, for the most part, been introduced into the high school literature classroom. As Applebee (1993) points out:

> The certainty of New Critical analysis has given way to formulations that force a more complex examination of the assumptions and expectations about authors, readers and texts as they are situated within specific personal and cultural contexts. The challenges to New Criticism, however, have taken place largely within the realm of literary theory. Only a few scholars have begun to give serious attention to the implications of these new approaches for classroom pedagogy . . . and most of that attention has been focused at the college level. It would be fair to say that, despite the recent ferment in literary theory, the majority of college undergraduates still receive an introduction to literature that has been little influenced by recent theory. (pp. 116–117)

In fact, Applebee (1993) found that 72% of the high school literature teachers he surveyed in schools that had a reputation for excellence "reported little or no familiarity with contemporary literary theory" (p. 122). As one high school teacher put it, "These are far removed from those of us who work on the front lines!" In one of the few texts about theory written explicitly for secondary teachers, Sharon Crowley (1989) agrees: "The practice of teaching people to read difficult and culturally influential texts is carried on, for the most part, as though it were innocent of theory, as though it were a knack that anybody could pick up by practicing it" (p. 26).

While it is not widely reflected in the practice of secondary teachers, the notion that literary theory can be useful for classroom teachers has gained greater voice in the field of English education. In *Literary Theory and English Teaching,* Griffith (1987) describes the tension between presenting literature as cultural artifacts or vehicles for transmitting ideology, and the aim of many educators, especially those who favor a more progressive approach to education, to use literature as a vehicle for self-exploration and expression. Griffith points out that the teaching of literary theory to secondary students is a useful way to bridge this gap:

> Certain applications of literary theory can lay bare what the text does not say and cannot say as well as what it does and, as part of the same process, to make certain aspects of the context in which the reading takes place visible as well.
> . . . To be able to offer pupils this sense of power over their environment seems a desirable goal, especially if the sense of power is more than a delusion and can lead in some way to an effect on the pupil's environment. (p. 86)

Dennie Palmer Wolf in *Reading Reconsidered* (1988) urges us to re-examine our notions of what literacy is, of what students should read, and of what it means to read well. She encourages us to teach students ways of thinking about texts. She writes, "Not to teach students these habits of mind would be to cheat them just as surely as if we kept them away from books written before 1900 and burned all poetry" (p. 4). Wolf reminds us that reading is "a profoundly social and cultural process" and urges us to provide all students with deeper and richer ways of thinking about literature, using terminology such as "holding a conversation with work," "becoming mindful," and "reading resonantly" (p. 9).

In *Textual Power: Literary Theory and the Teaching of English,* Robert Scholes (1985) argues that there are three basic textual skills: reading, interpretation, and criticism. Although there are many secondary English teachers skilled in all three, all too often they relegate only the reading to their students. It is they, rather than their students, who determine the appropriate critical approach for each literary text. After their critical stance has been

articulated, the teachers either allow students to create interpretations within the context of that critical approach or they provide a single privileged inter-pretation for the students. While the teacher may be well-schooled in theory, the students are not and therefore are limited in the interpretive choices they can make.

The call to theory has just begun to be heard by secondary school prac-titioners. As he contemplates the "shape high school literature should take in the coming years," Bruce Pirie (1997) also invokes Scholes (1985) as he calls for a repositioning of the study of literature that "clarifies its relation-ship with the rest of the world." Critics such as Scholes have pointed out that contemporary literary theory opens the barriers between the literary text and "the social text in which we live" (Scholes as quoted by Pirie, 1997, p. 31). It is at the opening, this intersection, of text and social context that the explicit study of contemporary literary theory can help adolescent readers make meaning of literary texts.

Kathleen McCormick, a scholar notable for her unique ability to grace-fully straddle the theoretical world of the university and the seemingly more pragmatic world of reading instruction in elementary and secondary schools, argues for the relevance of contemporary literary theories, especially those she calls "culturally informed theories," to the development of pedagogies in schools. She writes:

> While so often the schools and universities seem quite separate, it is primarily the research carried on in the colleges and universities that drives the reading lessons students are given in the schools. If feminists, theorists of race and gen-der and cultural studies, teachers, and researchers in the universities were to begin to engage in more active dialogue with the developers of reading programs and the teachers who have to teach students—young and older—"how" to read, it might be possible to begin to change the dominant significations of reading in the schools—so that more students could begin to learn to read the world simultaneously with learning to read the word—so that readers can begin to see themselves as interdiscursive subjects, to see texts as always "in use," and to recognize that different ways of reading texts have consequence. (1995, p. 308)

McCormick's suggestion that theoried ways of reading have significant consequences for our students of literature echoes an eloquent plea Janet Emig made a decade ago for the teaching of literary theory. In a conference paper as president-elect of the National Council of Teachers of English, Emig (1990) wrote, "Theory then becomes a vivid matter of setting out the beliefs that we hold against the beliefs of others, an occasion for making more coherent to others, and quite as important to ourselves, just what it is we believe, and why" (p. 93).

Emig underscores the power of the approach to teaching literature that will be presented in this book. The purpose of teaching literary theory at the secondary level is not to turn adolescents into critical theorists; rather, it is to encourage adolescents to inhabit theories comfortably enough to construct their own readings and to learn to appreciate the power of multiple perspectives. Literary theory can help secondary literature classrooms become sites of constructive and transactive activity where students approach texts with curiosity, authority, and initiative.

CRITICAL ENCOUNTERS IN HIGH SCHOOL ENGLISH offers instructional approaches that begin to meet the important challenge that Emig (1990) offered to her fellow teachers: "We must not merely permit, we must actively sponsor those textual and classroom encounters that will allow our students to begin their own odysseys toward their own theoretical maturity" (p. 94).

QUESTIONS ADDRESSED

CRITICAL ENCOUNTERS IN HIGH SCHOOL ENGLISH addresses some of the following questions:

- Which contemporary theories seem best-suited or most age-appropriate to high school students? Are some more "teachable" than others?
- What are some specific strategies that teachers can use to encourage multiple perspectives as students read literary texts?
- What does a teacher need to know about theory in order to be able to teach it?
- Is theory really relevant to marginalized or "at-risk" students, or is it only appropriate for college-track classrooms?
- Can the study of literary theory help students understand, question, and bridge cultural differences?
- How does the teaching of theory change classroom practice?
- What sorts of texts can be used in teaching contemporary literary theory?

ORGANIZATION OF BOOK

This book combines theory with actual classroom practice. It combines argument with narrative. Classroom examples illustrate the practice of teaching literary theory. Portraits of urban, suburban, and rural classrooms help make the case for particular theories. Throughout the book, actual lessons and

materials provide ways of integrating critical lenses into the study of literature. A variety of texts—"classics" such as *Hamlet, The Awakening, Of Mice
and Men, Heart of Darkness, Frankenstein,* and *The Great Gatsby,* as well as
titles that have been included in our secondary literature curriculum more
recently, such as *Beloved,* "The Yellow Wallpaper," *The Things They Carried,*
and *Native Son*—are used to illustrate a variety of literary lenses.

Chapter 1 sets forth the reasons for teaching critical theory, and Chapter
2 argues for the importance of multiple theoretical perspectives in reading
and interpreting literary texts. In Chapter 2, four very different classroom
vignettes illustrate the power of multiple perspectives. The vignettes suggest
specific strategies for introducing the notion of multiple perspectives to students (and to teachers) using several short stories and poems. These introductory activities, designed for students in grades 9–12, can be used at the beginning of a semester, trimester, or year-long course, or at the beginning of a
specific unit on critical analysis. The focus of the activities is on the power
of viewing literary texts from a variety of perspectives, not on specific literary
theories—yet. The emphasis on multiple perspectives and multiple ways of
viewing texts helps set the stage for the introduction of theories that constitute the rest of the book.

Is reader response an appropriate interpretive strategy for all students?
Is it useful or appropriate for all texts? Chapter 3 explores what happens
when students are taught how to apply the basic tenets of reader response
to their own reading. By describing what happens when students are given
interpretive tools that are explicitly named, this chapter demonstrates that
making teaching strategies explicit to students strengthens their interpretive
possibilities. This chapter also challenges some of the common assumptions
and practices of response-centered teaching, especially as they relate to diverse classrooms.

Chapter 4 explores the political prism of Marxist literary theory. This
chapter makes the case for the importance of political theory and argues that
Marxist literary theory may be best-suited to help students learn to understand, read, and perhaps even resist prevailing ideology. Texts such as *Of
Mice and Men, Black Boy, Native Son, Hamlet, The Great Gatsby,* and *Beloved*
also explore how these theoretical lenses help readers understand the political, social, and economic dimensions of the world in which we live.

Feminist literary theory is the focus of Chapter 5. The chapter explores,
through a series of classroom vignettes, a variety of pedagogical approaches
using feminist literary theory. Classroom situations are presented in which
students learn to interpret texts such as *A Doll's House, The Great Gatsby, A
Room of One's Own, The Awakening,* "The Yellow Wallpaper," *Frankenstein,*
and a variety of poetry using a feminist lens. Chapter 5 also looks at the
resistance both male and female students have to reading literary texts

through a feminist lens and illustrates how students can not only read literary texts through the prism of feminist theory but also learn to read the world through that refractive light.

Chapter 6 tackles a more difficult and even more rarely used contemporary theory, deconstruction. Students contrast the purposes of critical theories that are structural and linguistic with more political, extrinsic critical lenses. In using these theories, students are encouraged to focus on the specific language of literary texts (mostly poetry) and apply recent postmodern theories to those texts. Again, several specific lessons are provided to teachers, along with a discussion of the potential value of these approaches to high school students.

Chapter 7 describes how the teaching of literary theory dramatically affected a particular teacher's method of instruction. When she relinquished her position as literary authority in one class, she discovered that all of her classes became less teacher-centered and more exploratory. Excerpts from the teacher's journal chart her own personal and pedagogical transformation. In addition, the story of this unique teacher/researcher collaboration presents a potential model for alternative approaches to curriculum development, in-service training, and teacher education.

In addition to presenting concluding remarks, Chapter 8 summarizes the central thesis of the book: that literary theory can and should be taught to secondary students. Using literary theory as they read texts enables students to become theoried and skilled readers with a variety of interpretive strategies and theoretical approaches. As they become constructors of meaning, with multiple literary visions of their own, they become adept at reading the world around them.

Beyond providing portraits of particular teachers and students who embarked on this theoretical odyssey, this book offers teachers many specific teaching strategies for incorporating critical lenses into their literature curriculum. Included in the appendix are all of the activities that are described throughout the text. Teachers should feel free to adapt and use these activities in their own classrooms.

Through the Looking Glass: Introducing Multiple Perspectives

A man with one theory is lost. He needs several of them, or lots! He should stuff them in his pockets like newspapers.

—Bertolt Brecht

OPENING THE CLASSROOM DIALOGUE—FOUR VIGNETTES

"My Papa's Waltz"

Joe, a tenth-grade language arts teacher in an urban school, distributes Theodore Roethke's frequently anthologized poem "My Papa's Waltz" (see page 13) to his mixed-ability class of high school juniors. He asks them to read the poem to themselves several times and waits for the silence to be broken by the stirring of students ready to talk. In a series of gently prodding questions, he asks the class to construct an oral reading of the poem that conveys its meaning. One student, Mark, offers that it is a wistful remembrance of a young boy's affectionate kitchen romps with his deceased father. Joe asks the student to read the poem aloud with this interpretation in mind and he does so. His changing voice does not betray him as he reads gently and affectionately, stressing words like *papa, waltz, cling,* and so forth.

Complimenting the student on his reading, Joe turns to the rest of the class and peppers them with questions. "Is this the definitive reading?" he asks. "Is this what Roethke meant to communicate? Would all of you have read the poem the way Mark did, or are there any other ways this poem could be read?"

Slowly, hesitantly, a hand rises from the corner of the room. Marnie, a serious and quiet student, says firmly, "I don't think this poem is about a happy childhood recollection at all." Then under her breath, almost inaudibly, she asserts, "I think his dad was a drunk who beat him." Some members

of the class murmur in assent. Mark silently shakes his head in vigorous disagreement. Joe pushes. "How would the poem sound if that were the case? How would it be read? Does anyone care to try?" There are more than a few students who seem willing to take on this reading. Marnie is not one of them.

Josh begins to read forcefully:

The whisky on your breath
could make a small boy dizzy
But I hung on like death
Such waltzing was not easy.

We romped until the pans
Slid from the kitchen shelf
My mother's countenance
Could not unfrown itself.

The hand that held one wrist
Was battered on one knuckle
At every step you missed
My right ear scraped a buckle.

You beat time on my head
With a palm caked hard by dirt
Then waltzed me off to bed
Still clinging to your shirt.
                        —Theodore Roethke

He emphasizes words like *beat, death, battered, missed, dirt, whisky,* and so on. After the reading, some students in the room seem to shudder visibly from the effect of Josh's reading. They also seem a bit unsettled. Hadn't they already heard a convincing and sensible reading?

"Which one is right?" one student asks. "How do we know which way to read it?"

"Could they both be right ?" Joe asks.

"Not at the same time," one student replies.

"Not to the same person," another one offers.

"But do they both seem to make sense? Do they offer two plausible perspectives?" Amid general murmurs of assent, Joe continues. "There clearly seem to be more than two ways to read this poem, more than two ways to read the situation. This may turn out to be true for many of the texts we read together, as well as for many of the things that happen to us in everyday life." Joe smiles and hands out another poem, "Thirteen Ways of Looking at a Blackbird."

"Little Miss Muffet" and Other Tales

Bob, a veteran of 20 years of teaching, surveys his class of restless tenth graders, a varied assortment of children very different from the advanced placement students he generally is used to teaching. In the class are hard-working students who hope to go to college, a few students who are struggling to pass their classes, and a few underachieving students who long ago decided to get off the train of the college-prep track.

The students have read a short piece by essayist Russell Baker entitled "Little Miss Muffet" (see Appendix, Activity 1). Baker recasts the familiar fairy tale of the unfortunate Ms. Muffet and the intruding spider by retelling it through a variety of perspectives, for example, from the eyes of a psychiatrist, a teacher, a militarist, a child. The students respond ambivalently to the essay. They are surprised that anything as childish as a nursery rhyme is being introduced by a teacher who has a school-wide reputation for "making you think without making you sweat." Bob arranges the students into groups. Once in their groups, he asks them to select a nursery rhyme and recast it from several occupations or roles. The students do so and come back to class the next day with fanciful results. Here are three examples:

"Humpty Dumpty": Prosecuting Attorney's Point of View

This whole incident is obviously a conspiracy. There is no way Mr. Dumpty would just fall off the wall. Being in the fragile state that he was, he would have been extremely cautious while up on that wall. He was obviously distracted by a diversion so he wouldn't notice the suspect creeping up behind him, ready to push him off at just the right moment. It was just an "innocent fall" or so the members of the palace would have you believe. The fact of the matter is, all the king's horses and all the king's men are suspects. They all had a motive. They were sick and tired of the egg getting all the attention. And the fact that they couldn't put Mr. Dumpty back together is very suspicious, since they were all trained in egg life saving. So far, they've come up with an alibi, but it won't hold. There are almost as many holes in their stories as there are in Mr. Dumpty's poor broken body. (Maggie)

"There Was an Old Woman Who lived in a Shoe":
Democrat's Point of View

This is, no doubt, a serious concern of ours in the United States of America. We are no longer living in a middle-class suburban home with a father, mother, two-and-a-half children, and a family pet. This

poor woman needs the federal government's help. With a welfare check every so often, maybe she could feed her children something more nutritious than broth. And she's living in a shoe! What is happening to low-income housing these days? The government should raise some taxes so that she doesn't have to live in a shoe! Something that is so truly heartbreaking is that this poor mother is single and stuck with the burden of the children with no support from the father. We need to catch these absentee fathers and make them pay child support. Welfare not workfare is the answer to all of the Old Woman Who Lived in a Shoe's problems. (Mandi)

"Jack Be Nimble": Fire Chief's Point of View

This is a textbook example of what happens when fire is in the hands of careless children. Children should never play with fire. It's a cardinal rule. Everybody knows that. This isn't play. No, it's much worse than that; fire is not a toy. What we see developing is a blatant disrespect for the animal which is fire. We may be looking at a future arsonist of America. And, what's that candle doing on the floor in the first place? It's a fire hazard, people! (Eric)

When the reading of these new versions of nursery rhymes winds down, Bob reads aloud *The True Story of the 3 Little Pigs, by A. Wolf* (Scieszka, 1999), a children's book that retells the familiar tale from the point of view of the wolf. It begins: "Everybody knows the story of The Three Little Pigs. Or at least they think they do. But I'll let you in on a little secret. Nobody knows the real story, because nobody has ever heard *my* side of the story." And it ends: "So they jazzed up the story with all of that 'Huff and puff and blow your house down.' And they made me the Big Bad Wolf. That's it. The real story. I was framed."

Amid giggles and chatter, Jessie blurts out what many of his classmates were thinking, "Why did we do this, Mr. B? It was fun, but it seemed pointless."

"We did it to demonstrate one very important point—that the same story, even a simple story such as Little Miss Muffet, can take on very different meaning depending on who is doing the telling. So, when we read, the meaning depends on who's doing the reading. Meanings are constructed: We create meanings that are influenced by who we are and what we are culturally, historically, psychologically, and, in the case of the Baker versions of Miss Muffet, vocationally. If we can construct and change the meaning for something as simple as Little Miss Muffet, can you imagine the changes, the varia-

tions in meaning that occur among us as we read poems, short stories, and novels?"

"What if," Bob wonders aloud, "*The Adventures of Huckleberry Finn* were told from the perspective of Tom Sawyer or Jim; *To Kill a Mockingbird* were told from the perspective of Boo Radley or Tom Robinson; *The Diary of Anne Frank* from the point of view of Peter, Miep Giess, or Anne's father? How does a story change when the narrator changes? How are the basic elements of that story transformed? Is it the same story, or narrative, told from a different point of view, or does it become, at some point, a different story?"

Bob raises some questions fundamental to the study of literature, questions he would like to pursue with his students through the use of literary theory. How can we read a narrative from a single perspective and be able to trace the influences of that perspective on how the text is shaped? Given one perspective, how might we be able to imagine how other perspectives might change the telling of that narrative? In other words, how can we see the wolf's side in the pigs' story? Further, how can we deconstruct the singular vision that is represented by one story? And, how can we extrapolate from that single tile of vision to the mosaic of other human experiences and perspectives?

Imagine! All this from fairy tales and nursery rhymes!

In Search of Multiple Perspectives

Rachel is in her first year of teaching in a small rural community. Overall, her teaching has been going fairly well—she feels well-planned and well-prepared, and, for the most part, she's been able to maintain the interest of her ninth and tenth graders. Each day brings her a greater understanding of the different sensibilities between her small-town students and her own adolescence in a large, metropolitan city. Rachel admires the feeling of community and camaraderie among her students. There seems to be more unanimity about issues than she ever imagined possible in the diverse urban high school she attended. While she embraces the harmony of her students' common outlook, she finds the homogeneity of opinion tends to stifle class discussions. Like today.

After the class read *The Scarlet Letter*, Rachel held a final discussion that she hoped would arouse some controversy. Throughout their reading of the text (mandated by the district's curriculum), Rachel tried to present a variety of contestable issues. What is a moral code? Who were the characters they most and least admired? Did Hester deserve her fate? What motivated the townspeople—cruelty, morality, both? What is innocence? Who was using whom? Do we have absolute moral codes in today's society?

On a variety of occasions, she threw out several provocative statements,

playing devil's advocate and even offering some possible interpretations that
she knew her students would find implausible. But her playful questioning
was returned by either silence or half-hearted acquiescence. She tried ex-
tending one student's commentary by asking if anyone disagreed, but there
were no takers. Finally, in desperation and in probably what was not her
finest teaching moment she cried, "Isn't there *any* other way to see this? Do
we have only one point of view out there? How can that be? Counting me,
there are 31 of us. There has got to be more than one opinion among us!"

Rachel wants her students to be able to understand that there is usually
more than one side to any issue. Events, in literature and in life, are multifac-
eted and have different sides, cast different light, depending on the viewer.
She wants to change the monochrome of students' vision; she wants them to
see other perspectives. She hopes that by the end of their year together, students will be able to do more than walk around in someone else's shoes. They
should be able to see things from other viewpoints, heartily argue positions
that they don't believe in, inhabit other ways of being or habits of mind. She
wants her students to analyze their lives and texts, not just from the inside
out but from the outside in. Eventually she hopes that the students will be
able to take different theoretical stances to literary texts as well as other
things. But now, at the very least, she wants them to see that every story,
every position has more than one side. But, where should she begin?

She begins with the idea of being able to consider a story from the van-
tage point of a variety of perspectives, not simply the protagonist's. For Rachel, this is not simply an important step in interpretive reading; real life also
means looking beyond one's own point of view to understand the point of
view of someone else. Rachel chooses a story by John Updike called "Separating." It's a typical Updike story, set in suburbia, told from the husband's
point of view—and told as if there were no other point of view that mattered.
This myopic narration is particularly relevant to the story line (as well as
Rachel's larger purposes); the husband has decided to leave his wife, but
neither his wife nor his children are aware of the decision.

After her students read the story, Rachel asks them to consider the plot
of the story from the perspective of the other characters such as the wife or
the children (see Appendix, Activity 2). Rachel and her students move the
discussion of point of view (something with which they've been familiar since
seventh grade) into a discussion of world view or stance. She tells her students that stories often are told from a vision as singular as the husband; it's
just not always so painfully obvious to us. She tells them that for every text
they read, there is another tale wanting to be told, lurking behind the apron
strings of the narrator and author. Our job is to invoke those other voices,
always on the lookout for the betrayed wife, the neglected child, the overarching commentary about manicured lawns and cul-de-sacs. She tells them to

think about how tales could turn on the teller as they read their next book together, *Catcher in the Rye*.

Star Wars

It is a crisp, September morning and the school year is only 2 weeks old. The students in Martha's twelfth-grade advanced placement class have just finished reporting on their summer reading. They are beginning to get to know each other and their teacher and are trying to figure out how this last year of high school English, how this advanced placement class, may be different from their previous study of literature. Or will it be? In *Literature in the Secondary School* Applebee (1993) reports on how little has changed in curriculum and instruction in most high school literature classrooms, especially among the upper-track classes. Are Martha's students simply in for more of the same?

On this particular day, the classroom is darkened and the students absolutely cannot believe their good fortune. The teacher has popped *Star Wars* into the VCR. She asks them to just jot down a few things that strike them as particularly interesting or important as they view the film. Despite the block scheduling, the film spills into the next period and Martha feels a little guilty. After all, this *is* advanced placement and the students' parents and administrators seem to impose a different level of accountability on the class.

When the film is over and the lights come on, Martha waits for the students to piece back together their location in the classroom world of fluorescent lights and chalk dust, literally light years from the intergalactic battles they've been cheering on. Martha distributes a discussion sheet entitled "Theory Wars" (see Appendix, Activity 3). Together they discuss the first two questions. They discuss the relative merits of seeing a movie and of reading a book more than once. They weigh the advantage of the surprise and spontaneity of a first reading or viewing to the ability to see things one didn't see the first time, during a second, more considered reading. They also discuss the relative inequities that often exist in most classroom settings when students are encountering a text for the first time and the teacher may be encountering it for the tenth or thirtieth time (Rabinowitz, 1987).

Martha leads the students through a brief discussion about archetypes, and the students are visibly gleeful about how easily the archetypes they learned last year in British Literature class seem to fit the characters of *Star Wars*. Martha takes a deep breath and hands out a sheet called "Literary Theories: A Sampling of Critical Lenses" (see Appendix, Activity 4). This handout contains brief synopses of some of the major literary theories she hopes to include during the rest of the year. It is a dynamic document, changing each year with a collective reconsideration of theory by Martha and her

students. At this early stage of their time together, Martha does not want to either overwhelm or overfeed the class; she simply wants to give them a preview or taste of the theories to come and then reintroduce them, weaving them into the curriculum as the year progresses.

Generally, none of Martha's students has heard of literary theory before. Even though (as discussed in Chapter 1) many of them have been in classrooms that favor either a New Critical or a reader-response approach, those responses have never been explicitly articulated or "named." Their study of literature, to this point, has been atheoretical. One could argue that, even for this upper track, their entire education has been atheoretical. That is, the biases that frame the particular perspectives of their learning—whether scientific paradigms, historical school of thought, or approaches to literature—have never been admitted. To be sure, however, they are at play in the presentation of knowledge as truth. The students deserve to know that. They also need the tools that will help them recognize and evaluate the ideologies through which their education has been funneled. As Stephen Bonnycastle (1996) points out:

> The main reason for studying theory at the same time as literature is that it forces you to deal consciously with the problem of ideologies. . . . If you are going to live intelligently in the modern world, you have to recognize that there are conflicting ideologies and that there is no simple direct access to the truth. (p. 19)

Martha knows the dangers of teaching didactically; she tends to prefer a more inductive or discovery approach, but this brief but explicit introduction of a sampling of literary theories is part of her grand plan. She hopes to briefly introduce all of the literary theories at once, to just let them simmer in the students' minds as she introduces the readings and the texts one by one over the course of the school year. Martha and her students will return to this sheet again and again as they reframe their reading into the multiple perspectives that are suggested by the theories. Herein lies the optometrist's gold—the treasure trove of different-colored lenses that can alter our vision. Martha and her class have taken the first step into their theoretical odyssey, an odyssey that is at the very center of her curriculum for her advanced placement students and the center of this book.

WHAT'S NEW ABOUT THEORY

These four vignettes, although they take place in separate classrooms distinguished by significant differences in teachers, students, and curriculum, pro-

vide an opening salvo to the concept of multiple perspectives. The activities themselves can be used individually or they can occur consecutively in any classroom. I tend to use all four when I introduce the topic of multiple perspectives and do them roughly in the order in which I present them here (Appleman, 1993). As argued below, encouraging multiple perspectives provides a conceptual introduction to considering the different "readings" of a text that literary theory can provide.

Taken together, these activities help students understand that literature can be read from a variety of perspectives. This pluralistic approach indicates that the sources of these different perspectives do not always spring from personal experience. It encourages students to hold texts up to the light like a prism just to see how many colors might be cast. Or, to return to the opening metaphor from the introduction, it offers readers a variety of tinted lenses through which they can view things differently.

At first blush, the experienced literature teacher may wonder if we are really offering anything new. For example, many teachers may have used "My Papa's Waltz" to teach tone. Activities such as rewriting nursery rhymes or considering other characters in the Updike story help teachers convey age-old literary devices such as point of view, protagonist, or characterization. Similarly, archetypes, such as those embedded in Martha's *Star Wars* activity, have formed the anatomy of our literary criticism for years.

Further, the notion that there are several critical stances or perspectives from which texts can be viewed is no stranger to the language arts curriculum, especially a literature curriculum that has been duly influenced by Louise Rosenblatt, Robert Probst, and other notable proponents of reader response. Reader response clearly claims that the meaning of texts changes from reader to reader, that there is no single "correct" interpretation, that it is created by the transaction of reader and text, and that every reader may create a different interpretation of a text, given our different backgrounds and orientations. Yet all reader responses, regardless of how they may vary from student to student and reader to reader, are really variations on a single theoretical theme: that personal experiences provide the lens that colors the reading of the text. There is, of course, some unassailable truth as well as pedagogical promise to this claim. But there are many theoretical approaches other than reader response that rarely are used in secondary literature classrooms. Additionally, as literature teachers we may want to move students beyond their own personal response into the perspective of others. As Pirie (1997) points out, "At some point, examination of their own meaning-making will probably lead students to recognize limitations in their current perspectives—that's a characteristic of growth, after all—and engender new appreciation of many things, including perhaps Shakespeare" (p. 23).

Teaching multiple approaches to literature through contemporary liter-

ary theory promotes what many in the field of literacy education have come to regard as a constructivist approach to literature. As Applebee (1993) defines constructivism, "Instruction becomes less a matter of transmittal of an objective and culturally sanctioned body of knowledge, and more a matter of helping individual learners learn to construct and interpret for themselves." Applebee goes on to say that "the challenge for educators is how in turn to embed this new emphasis into the curricula they develop and implement" (pp. 200–201). When teachers introduce literary theory into their literature classes, they invite students to construct both interpretive method and literary meaning into their study of literature. No longer will students respond within a preselected theoretical paradigm. They construct the theoretical context as well as the content of their meaning making.

THE END OF THE BEGINNING

After these initial introductory activities, some teachers might want to offer students some straightforward explications of literary theory, such as Stephen Lynn's "A Passage into Critical Theory" (1990), an essay in which he interprets a story by Brendan Gill about working at the *New Yorker* from a variety of theoretical perspectives. The essay nicely iterates the structure of the Baker piece but pushes students more firmly into the direction of theory. Excerpts from *The Pooh Perplex* by Frederick C. Crews (1965) provide a more elaborate variation on the same theme. These pieces whimsically demonstrate how different theoretical perspectives cast light differently on the same text, even an "innocent text" such as *Winnie the Pooh*. And, they remind all of us of the potential absurdity that can result when we overreach with our criticism:

> The fatal mistake that has been made by every previous Pooh-ologist is the confusion of Milne the writer with Milne the narrator, and of Christopher Robin the listener with Christopher Robin the character. These are not two personages but four, and no elementary understanding of Pooh is possible without this realization. We must designate, then, the Milne within the story as "the Milnean voice" and we must call the Christopher Robin who listens "the Christopheric ear." With these distinctions in mind, Pooh begins to make perfect sense for the first time. (Crews, 1965, p. 6)

Humor and grace are important in this enterprise, for the introduction of theory needs to be approached gently and with care. Students already suspect that we English teachers meet together at conferences and make up terms like tone, symbol, and protagonist just so we can trick them on the next test, wreck something that was just starting to seem like fun, or complicate

something that was just starting to get more simple. If theory is going to be believed and used by students, if it is somehow going to become an integral part of their repertoire of reading, then it needs a chance to make a case for itself, even if that means beginning slowly and subtly with activities such as the ones used by Joe, Bob, Rachel, and Martha.

Clearly not every theory should be used with every text. Reading with theory can become as mechanistic and arbitrary as some of the other kinds of literary apparatuses we've been collectively guilty of overusing in the past. Applying theory should be neither mandatory nor automatic. In fact, as Susan Sontag (1969) has argued, the reading of some texts should be done without any theory or interpretation at all. I sometimes go weeks without directly applying theory, letting it lie fallow as we go about our reading in the usual way. More often than not, as we read together, a student may bring up a particular lens. When that happens, I know that their theoretical journey is progressing, that it is they and not I alone who help construct the theoretical framework of the classroom.

While a teacher may chart the theoretical journey anywhere and with any theory or combination of theories, in this book we begin our study of theory with the one with which students may have the most practice—reader response. Although in many classrooms students have become well-socialized into sharing their personal responses to texts, rarely have they heard of Louise Rosenblatt or have they any idea that their responses lie within a particular theoretical framework. Additionally, reader response often is unconditionally presented to students as the most comfortable and familiar way into a text, even though many teachers, like Rachel, have some understanding of the limitations and perhaps even dangers of this particular pedagogical approach, what Pirie (1997) calls "the cult of the individual." It is time to pull back the curtain on the workings of reader response.

SUGGESTED ADDITIONAL READING
General Works on Literary Theory (Chapters 1 and 2)

Bloom, H. (1994). *The Western canon: The books and school of the ages.* New York: Harcourt.

  Through his analysis of 26 major writers, Bloom traces the Western literary tradition. Borges, Chaucer, George Eliot, Goethe, Shakespeare, and Tolstoy are a few of the writers whom he analyses. Bloom argues against the place of ideology in literary criticism, but he also offers/eschews arguments for Marxism, feminism, new historicism, poststructuralism, and other critical lenses.

Bonnycastle, S. (1996). *In search of authority: An introductory guide to literary theory* (2nd ed.). Peterborough, Ontario: Broadview Press.

A lively and thought-provoking introduction to a variety of theories. Bonny-castle focuses on the role reading with theory can play in helping readers learn to recognize and resist ideology.

Carpenter, S. (2000). *Reading lessons: An introduction to theory.* Upper Saddle River, NJ: Prentice-Hall.
    This unusual book focuses on the playful quality of reading with theory. It draws its examples from popular culture as well as from familiar literary texts. Written with college students in mind, its engaging style makes it useful for both teachers and advanced high school students.

Childers, J., & Hentzi, G. (Eds.). (1995). *The Columbia dictionary of modern literary and cultural criticism.* New York: Columbia University Press.
    This is written for the general reader who wants a concise and usable definition of the theoretical terms and concepts used in the field of cultural and literary criticism, making criticism in these fields available and theoretical arguments understandable.

Herron, J. et al. (Eds.). (1986). *The ends of theory.* Detroit: Wayne State University Press.
    This collection of 16 essays by prominent contributors from a variety of disci-plines sheds light on the past 3 decades of debate about theory. It has sections on critics and criticism, aims and ends of literature, and aesthetics and poetics.

Hogan, P. C. (1990). *The politics of interpretation: Ideology, professionalism, and the study of literature.* Oxford: Oxford University Press.
    Hogan draws on a variety of theoretical positions such as Marxist, feminist, psychoanalytic, and Derridian perspectives. He offers an interpretive study of the politics of literature, criticism, and professionalism.

Lentricchia, F., & McLaughlin, T. (Eds.). (1995). *Critical terms for literary study.* Chicago: University of Chicago Press.
    An excellent reference tool described as a "landmark introduction" to the world of literary theory, this work is a collection of essays that explore the concepts that shape how we read literature and help the reader understand literary works as results of cultural practices.

Lynn, S. (1998). *Texts and contexts: Writing about literature with critical theory* (2nd ed.). New York: Longman.
    This book is an excellent introduction to several major literary theories, includ-ing deconstruction, reader response, feminist criticism, New Criticism, psycho-logical criticism, and biographical, historical, and new historical criticism. Lynn provides strategies not only for reading but for writing about literature using these theories.

Marakaryk, I. R. (1993). *Encyclopedia of contemporary literary theory: Approaches, scholars, terms.* Toronto: University of Toronto Press.

This volume is a collection of efforts of scholars from various departments at universities across the continent—religion, philosophy, sociology, linguistics, political science, to name a few—offering a rich variety of viewpoints of contemporary theory. The collection also includes important precursors to the theories, giving the reader complete and grounded building blocks for the study of literary theory.

Peck, J., & Coyle, M. (1993). *Literary terms and criticism.* London: Macmillan.

In this new, expanded edition of their original 1984 work, Peck and Coyle provide the reader with updated, insightful commentary discussing traditional criticism, feminist criticism, Marxist criticism, New Criticism, Russian formalism, narratology, phenomenological criticism, psychoanalytic criticism, reader-response theory, structuralism, poststructuralism, deconstruction, and New Historicism.

Selden, R. (1989). *Practicing theory and reading literature: An introduction.* Lexington: Kentucky University Press.

This work is a general, resourceful collection with explanatory sections on such critical approaches as feminism, Marxism, formalism, structuralism, and reader response.

The Lens of Reader Response: The Promise and Peril of Response-Based Pedagogy

What a poem means is the outcome of a dialogue between the words on the page and the person who happens to be reading it; that is to say, its meaning varies from person to person.

—W. H. Auden

We must keep clearly in mind that the literary experience is fundamentally an unmediated private exchange between a text and a reader, and that literary history and scholarship are supplemental.

—Robert Probst, *Response and Analysis*

A poem is the map of a dream.

—Kevin, Grade 12

This poem has no meaning to me. Because I get no meaning, it is not poetry.

—Jesse, Grade 12

A FEW YEARS AGO I served as an "invigilator" for an International Baccalaureate program in an urban high school in Minneapolis. My role as an outside examiner was to help students demonstrate their understanding of several canonical texts (*Oedipus Rex, Macbeth, Hamlet, The Grapes of Wrath, The Scarlet Letter*) by asking them first to prepare a brief explication of the text and then to respond to a series of questions.

Particularly memorable was one discussion I had about *The Scarlet Letter* with a 16-year-old student named Leah. Leah spent about two or three sentences on plot summary and then exclaimed, "You know, if my man ever treated me the way Hester's man treated her, he'd be out of my life before you could say 'The Scarlet A.' I can't believe the crap Hester took. Actually,

last week my boyfriend Rob and I almost broke up. Okay, well, it all started when. . ."

Try as I might, I couldn't move our conversation back to Hester or to anything specifically textual about *The Scarlet Letter* or any of the other texts she had read for her IB English course. I felt that she had dived off the springboard of personal response into an autobiographical wreck (apologies to Adrienne Rich). Leah's inability to craft a response that was textual in any way might have been facilitated inadvertently by her skilled and well-meaning teacher who encouraged personal responses to literature and de-emphasized more traditional forms of textual analysis. While this anecdote may exaggerate the "worst case scenario" of the personalized approach to literature, it does point out some of the potential weaknesses in how that approach has come to be practiced in secondary schools.

This chapter reviews some of the basic tenets of a *reader-centered* approach, discusses some of the many advantages of this particular lens, and explains how its practice may have diverted from its intentions. We then explore some of the limitations to the approach that have emerged recently as both students and canon have become more diverse. Finally, a close look at reader-response activities in two different classrooms reveals that we can use reader response with our students more fruitfully by (1) teaching it more explicitly, and (2) teaching it as one of a variety of theoretical approaches rather than as the only possible approach. This multiplicity of approaches will be explored further in subsequent chapters.

BENEFITS OF THE READER-CENTERED APPROACH

There can be no denying the power and purpose of a reader-centered approach to literature and the degree to which it has positively informed our practice. It has made the enterprise of literature teaching more relevant, immediate, and important. It has forced us to rethink what we do when we teach literature, why we do it, and whom we do it for. There is ample evidence of the soundness of the reader-centered approach; its advocates are influential and articulate—from Rosenblatt's efferent to aesthetic reading to Langer's engagement with literature to Robert Probst's elegant and elegiac meditations on the importance of personal response. The value of the lens of reader response to literature study in secondary classrooms simply cannot be denied. And no one would want to.

As we look back at literature instruction over the past half century, it is easy to see how reader-centered teaching fit perfectly with the goals of constructivist education and with the progressive education movement. At the center of the educational enterprise was the student. No longer was the

text itself or the author the most salient part of literature study. No longer could students' individual responses to texts be considered "mnemonic irrelevancies," as I. A. Richards had claimed. Instead, the reader was the creator of meaning through a "never to be duplicated transaction" between the reader and the text (Rosenblatt, 1968, p. 31).

This new focus on the reader indisputably enlivened and irrevocably altered the teaching of literature. It changed or supposedly changed the power dynamics in the classroom and the role of the teacher, and it clearly changed what it was that we asked students to do when they read texts. The paradigmatic shift from a text-centered to a reader-centered pedagogy also changed our consideration of the kinds of texts we used. We found ourselves sometimes considering whether a particular text was teachable by the degree to which it might invoke personal responses from our students. From the point of view of most observers, at least, these were all changes for the better.

Five-paragraph themes gave way to reading logs; recitations of genre or structural aspects of the text gave way to recitations of personal connections to the text; and the traditional teacher-in-the-front formation gave way to the intimate and misshapen circles with which many of us and our students are familiar. Of course, knowledge of the text was still important, but personal knowledge seemed in many cases to be privileged over textual knowledge. Rather than seeking out biographical information about the author or historical information about the times in which the text was written or took place, teachers began to spend time finding personal hooks into the texts they chose and frequently opened literature discussions with questions that began, "Have you ever . . . ?"

A CAUTIONARY TALE

We met Rachel in Chapter 2. Rachel was an enthusiastic, if relatively inexperienced, practitioner of reader-centered pedagogy and had become increasingly frustrated as she watched her students measure, by their own limited experiences, the predicaments and decisions of Hester Prynne, George and Lenny, Daisy Buchanan, and Atticus Finch. On the one hand, she is grateful that they can find connections between their own lives and the lives of these literary characters. She knows that personal experience often provides the coattails students ride into a book. She also knows enough about reader-response approaches to the teaching of literature from her college methods class to realize that using one's personal experiences to connect to the text can be a fruitful way for students to make meaning. She knows that personal response is the hook that many teachers favor for good reason. In fact, some of her colleagues contend it is the only way that really works.

And still . . . There is something about this personal approach to literature with which Rachel feels uncomfortable. Yes, she wants her students to read literature to gain insight into their own lives, to gain perspective into their own situations. Yet there is, Rachel believes, something limiting about that position, something that might trivialize the importance of the real differences that exist between the students' world and the world of the text. Are we *really* all the same? Is the purpose of studying literature only to clarify our own existence and underscore our unique personal attributes? We know the personal connection and engagement with literature that is gained when students measure the relationship of Hester and Chillingsworth through their own dating experiences, or measure issues of adultery with contemporary scandals involving American presidents. But what is lost?

Rachel is not the only one who has been reconsidering the relative merits of reader response. Perhaps one of the most biting reappraisals of an individualized reader-centered approach is offered by Bruce Pirie in *Reshaping High School English* (1997). In a chapter tellingly titled "Beyond Barney and the Cult of the Individual," Pirie reflects on the practice of valorizing individual responses in the literature classroom and the inherent dangers and complications of that approach. He argues that our focus on individuals may be overly simplistic. Even our definition of "individual" may be flawed; it does not acknowledge the contextual factors that help make us individuals. As English teachers we may have been guilty of overprivileging and romanticizing the individual at the expense of considerations of context. Pirie warns, "We now need to question the limits of the doctrine of individualism before our classroom practices harden into self-perpetuating rituals" (p. 9). This is, in part, what James Marshall (1991) refers to when he calls reader response our new orthodoxy.

Pirie notes Applebee's (1993) observation that we shuttle between valorizing personal response as an end in itself and using it as a hook or motivation to get students interested in more serious literary analysis. Pirie (1997) also questions whether a personal-response approach to literature is justifiable from the perspective of academic rigor: "I am, however, suspicious of the suggestion that just expressing your personal response is a satisfactory educational attainment, or that such a response could be evaluated for its authenticity" (p. 120).

This failure to critique readings is also lamented by Michael Smith (Smith and Rabinowitz, 1998) when he says, "I think it's important for readers and teacher to have a theoretical model that allows them to critique readings" (p. 121). In their provocative book *Authorizing Readers,* Smith and Rabinowitz remind us of the importance of authorial intention. If reader response is a transaction, at the very least we need to acknowledge that the text is an equal partner in that transaction. Meaning is a result of a kind of

negotiation between authorial intent and the reader's response. It is not simply the question, "What does this mean to me?" that Smith says captures the essence of reader-centered theories. How can literature foster a knowledge of others when we focus so relentlessly on ourselves and our own experiences? Without some attention to authorial readings, Smith and Rabinowitz remind us, we give up the power of the text to transform.

BE CAREFUL OF WHAT YOU ASK FOR; YOU JUST MIGHT GET IT

Perhaps the excesses that alarm even some of the originators and strongest supporters of reader-centered pedagogy have to do with how atheoretical its practice has become. Students are not exactly sure what it is they are supposed to do when they respond to a text; they just know they are supposed to respond *personally*. A cynical tenth grader once confided, "My teacher likes it when we get gooey and personal—the gooier, the better." They sometimes even overreact by saying things like Nathan did in an eleventh-grade discussion of *Snow Falling on Cedars*: "You really can't tell me anything about this book since my *personal* response is the only thing that counts." We may have "balkanized" the response-based classroom, thus precluding the possibility of questioning our personal experiences. Since our responses to literary texts are particularly and uniquely ours, then what is it that anyone, teacher or classmate, could offer that would either enrich or contradict them? Perhaps it is this phenomenon that frustrates Rachel so much when she tries to get a discussion going. Her students' attitude seems to be, "If my response is uniquely mine, then what can anyone else tell me about it?" This also leads to the sort of autobiographical diving that Leah did with *The Scarlet Letter* in the anecdote that opened this chapter. Bonnycastle (1996) addresses this issue of reader response when he writes: "If each of us only pays attention to individual experience, the communal basis for the discipline will disappear and literature classes will have nothing to hold them together" (p.174).

Then, of course, there is the matter of students who may be uncomfortable with personal response. This may be more than a question of learning style; it is in some ways a privacy issue or perhaps a cultural issue. The sharing circle that characterizes much of our practice is also culturally determined (Hynds & Appleman, 1997). It makes assumptions about the amount of trust that students have in each other and in their teachers. It makes some assumptions about their relationship to the institution of schooling and whether they have experienced school as a safe place. Perhaps most important, it also makes some assumptions about the degree to which students' lives are in "sharable shape." And, of course, underlying all of these assumptions is our belief that the sharing of personal responses in the public sphere of school

will bring students to a greater understanding of themselves and each other rather than underscore the depths of the chasms, of the inequality, that often divide us. This is the essence of the false promise of democracy in the literature circle.

CONFESSIONS OF A TRUE BELIEVER

As a high school teacher during the 1970s and 1980s, I was an enthusiastic practitioner of reader response. I tirelessly sought the personal connections that would engage my students with a text, whether it was *To Kill a Mockingbird, Of Mice and Men, Ordinary People, Black Boy, The Hobbit,* or *The Great Gatsby.* Like the teachers I described above, I began more than my share of literature discussions with that "Have you ever . . . ?" opening. I have to admit, however, that while I considered myself to be a true-blue reader-response teacher for about 10 years of high school teaching, I never once explained to the students that what we were doing was called "reader response." While I'm sure I explained or paraphrased the concept of a "transaction" with a literary text in general terms, I never was explicit about what exactly we were doing and why.

Sometimes the students themselves, noticing the tone of our classroom yet not being able to name the difference they felt, would refer obliquely or disparagingly to Ms. Engstrom's sophomore American literature class or Ms. Debarge's eleventh-grade British Literature class where there was clearly *one* meaning to a passage or even an entire text and feelings were *never* discussed. The students would reminisce bitterly about memorizing quotations, preparing for nit-picky objective tests, and embarking on wildly elusive symbol hunts. Even then I wasn't clear about what was different in this class. Neither did I name the competing traditions of literary study nor admit to myself and to my students the validity and potential advantages of a more text-centered approach. As I prepared my reader-friendly lessons, journal assignments, and essays, I vilified the New Critics, making them the evil straw people of single-minded interpretations. Ben Nelms (1988) stated it well in this description:

> I learned to think of the literary text as an edifice. Almost as a temple. Complete, autonomous, organically whole, sacrosanct. We approached it with reverence. We might make temple rubbings and we were encouraged to explain how its arches carried its weight and to speculate on the organic relationship between its form and function. But it was an edifice and we were spectators before its splendors. (p. 1)

I congratulated myself that I could never treat my students as "spectators" or the texts as "temples." I felt comfortable and confident in my reader-response pedagogy—even superior. Looking back, from the viewpoint of multiple perspectives, I realize I was guilty of imposing a theoretical framework with no room for deviation. In my own way, although I could never see it or admit it then, I was as narrow-minded and singular in my theoretical vision as Ms. Engstrom or Ms. Debarge and their single-answer worksheets and symbol hunts.

I would like to be able to claim that I somehow saw the light and eventually learned to teach explicitly and theoretically while I was a high school teacher, but that is simply not the case. It was only when I began teaching about teaching that I started making response-based teaching explicit with my own version of "the naming of parts." For those preservice and inservice teachers who had never been pricked by the needles of "porcupines making love" (Purves, Rogers, & Soter 1990), I began to think strategically about how to make the lens of reader response explicit. In other words, I didn't simply want to encourage my students to respond to literature within a classroom context that was never articulated; I wanted to teach them about the theory of reader response and then encourage them to respond to literary texts with those responses enriched by their metacognitive awareness of that theory.

PULLING BACK THE CURTAIN

I began to pull the curtain back on reader response with my secondary methods students and realized, as I had with many other instructional strategies, that I had been withholding from the high school students themselves the power of being able to name what it was that they were doing. It was rather like wanting students to reach the upper levels of Bloom's taxonomy but never teaching them about the taxonomy itself. I sometimes felt as if I had been teaching high school like the Wizard of Oz, trying to create magic and illusion, asking students to ignore the man behind the green curtain when all the time it would have been more illustrative and perhaps even more magical without the illusion, if I only had trusted them enough to take them backstage.

Taking them backstage wasn't very hard. While there are many different forms and variations of reader response—as Beach (1993) categorizes them, textual, social, psychological, cultural, and experiential—I decided to focus primarily on a version of Louise Rosenblatt's transactional approach. It is, in many ways, the most straightforward, sensible, and comprehensible to secondary students. And, thanks to the wonderful "translations" of Robert

Probst, it seems to be the version of a reader-centered approach to literature with which most secondary teachers are familiar. Rosenblatt views literary reading as a transaction between reader and text. She views responding to literature as an "event." As Richard Beach explains in his useful volume, *A Teacher's Introduction to Reader-Response Theories* (1993),

> In contrast to the textual theorists who are interested in the competent or ideal readers' knowledge in general, Rosenblatt focuses on the uniqueness of a particular momentary transaction. While the textual theorists are concerned with achieving interpretation consistent with knowledge of appropriate literary conventions, theorists adopting Rosenblatt's transactional model are open to exploring their responses as reflecting the particulars of their emotions, attitudes, beliefs, interests, etc. (p. 51)

Beach (1993) illustrates some of the principles of reader-response theory by using the poem "Mushrooms" by Sylvia Plath. The poem is so oblique and ambiguous that it can illustrate nicely some of the basic tenets of reader response for secondary students. It can become an important part of a lesson designed to help "pull back the curtain."

Mushrooms

Overnight, very
Whitely, discreetly,
Very quietly

Our toes, our noses
Take hold on the loam,
Acquire the air
Nobody sees us,
Stops us, betrays us;
The small grains make room.

Soft fists insist on
Heaving the needles,
The leafy bedding,

Even the paving.
Our hammers, our rams,
Earless and eyeless,

Perfectly voiceless,
Widen the crannies.
Shoulder through holes. We

Diet on water,
On crumbs of shadow.
Bland-mannered, asking

Little or nothing.
So many of us!
So many of us!

We are shelves, we are
Tables, we are meek,
We are edible.

Nudgers and shovers
In spite of ourselves.
Our kind multiplies:

We shall by morning
Inherit the earth.
Our foot's in the door.
                    —Sylvia Plath

As Beach reports, readers respond with marked variety to this text and construct a wide range of interpretations. When the poem is presented to students without its title, even more interesting variation can result. For example, some students divine that the poem is about some kind of vegetation (from moss to trees), while others, especially female students, have mentioned that they think it's about unborn babies. Some students have suggested that it's about people who are oppressed—either people of color or perhaps women. One student ingeniously suggested that the poem was about rabbits and provided a line-by-line explication using such words as *multiply, silent*, and *edible* to prove that it was so. A few others reported magical and mysterious walks in the woods with their fathers or mothers. Some even denoted a trace of mental illness in the poem.

Here are some of the responses of eleventh- and twelfth-grade students after they were asked to write their response to the poem on an index card:

This poem is about conformity and how it jeopardizes our individuality.

It's about making a place for yourself in the world. That, or mold.

This poem is about an oppressed group of people. They are beaten, ignored, abused, used. There is some hope of things being OK for them. It comes in inheriting the earth. They are almost there.

These are slaves, escaping from plantations. They were just mindless tools before; now they are individuals.

Snow.

About a class of unnoticed underdogs who will come together silently and rise against the present power.

Trees, about to be made into different material things.

It's about the working class of people and how there are many more of them than the higher, richer class.

The voice of vegetation in the spring.

White carpenter ants.

I do believe this poem is about the birth of man in this planet.

It is about the seeds of cottonwood trees being dispersed in the wind during the night. They float through the air and when they land they push their way into the soil and begin to grow.

I think this is a dream. A dream is the uninhibited imagination and a poem is the same thing put to words. A poem is the map of a dream.

Together we are everything and together we are nothing.

Insects, cockroaches . . . It made me think of how they say that if there is ever a nuclear war, it would just be cockroaches left to cover the earth.

Mushroom-rotting fungus plaguing the earth.

Perhaps a minority or an oppressed people speaking up for their rights, learning to come forward, finally be recognized.

This is about individuality.

It could be our souls inside our head.

It's about woodland mice.

As these statements demonstrate, the range of responses to this poem is extraordinary, although some kind of cohort pattern sometimes can be detected—more women tend to see the unborn babies; college students seem to be more likely to see oppression. Students are usually amazed at the diversity of responses, and the activity itself makes the case for the notion that

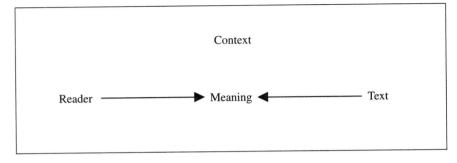

Figure 3.1 Reader-Response Diagram

our responses to literature are almost as individual as a kind of literary fingerprint.

It is at this point, after they've responded to "Mushrooms," that I introduce the reader-response diagram to secondary students (see Figure 3.1). This diagram graphically illustrates the principles of Rosenblatt's transactional theory of reader response in the following ways. First, students are asked to consider what personal characteristics, qualities, or elements of their personal histories might be relevant to their reading of a particular text. We stress that the relevant personal qualities or attributes they choose are dependent on the particular text. For example, it is obviously relevant that I have red hair when I consider my response to *Anne of Green Gables*. However, the fact that I have red hair is irrelevant when considering my responses to *A Separate Peace, All Quiet on the Western Front*, or *The Awakening*.

On the right side of the diagram, students are asked to consider the textual properties that might affect their reading or response and to list those properties. They might, for example, list the presence of vernacular or other aspects of vocabulary, the length of sentences, use of punctuation or italics, or the narrative structure. I point out to the students that all of these factors do contribute to a reader's response to a particular piece, but they are characteristics of the literary work, not of the individual reader.

In addition to considering both textual and personal characteristics, students also are asked to consider what contextual features may have influenced their reading. In some respects, adolescent readers seem to have a difficult time differentiating between the contextual and the personal, a fact that would not surprise most observers of adolescents. The lack of bound-

aries between self and other typifies the kind of adolescent egocentrism that David Elkind (1986) has described. In this case, the word *context* is used in a fairly narrow sense, as the context or conditions under which the book was read. For example, people read differently under the florescent light of the classroom or on an airplane in close proximity to a stranger than they do when they are in the comfort of their own home and their favorite reading place. The amount of homework, what one has been required to do as part of reading, and what else may be occurring at school or at home are all factors that contribute to the reading context.

Next, we apply the reader-response diagram to the students' responses to the poem "Mushrooms." On the left or reader side of the diagram, students often list their affinity or lack of affinity for nature, their comfort and experience with reading poetry, awareness of being part of an oppressed or marginalized group, and whatever prior knowledge they might have about the poem. On the right or textual side of the diagram, students may list the following textual properties: There are only one or two words per page, the language is very concrete, the poem doesn't rhyme, it's "modern" and imagistic. Sometimes they mention that the poem is written by Sylvia Plath and offer some biographical information or insights (just the kind of thing that drove those New Critics crazy).

After we describe the mechanics of the transaction or dialectic between reader and text, we further discuss how that dialectic created individual responses for the readers that enabled them to construct their own personal meaning for the text. Given the range of responses to "Mushrooms," it is easy for students to see how they have imprinted their own experiences and understandings onto the text itself and rendered interpretations as diverse as their own life experiences. At this point, the case for reader response generally makes itself. Now, let's see how pulling back the curtain plays out in two different classrooms with two different texts.

READER RESPONSE AND *RUNNING FIERCELY TOWARD A HIGH THIN SOUND:* "I AM NOT A LESBIAN; I AM NOT A JEW"

Carolyn Bell's advanced placement class quickly forms the large circle that is the *de rigueur* formation of the class. Located in one of the most diverse high schools in the city of Minneapolis, the class of 30 doesn't fully reflect the heterogeneity of the overall school population, but it is more diverse than many of the advanced placement or college-preparatory classes elsewhere in the state. Juniors and seniors, males and females, preppies and goths, White students and students of color, brown hair, blue hair, yellow hair, jocks and poets, gays, straights, and bisexuals, they all assemble in their delicious and

unpredictable individuality. Their regular teacher is a skilled and imaginative veteran with a taste for offbeat literature and a deep faith in her students' ability to be engaged and adventurous readers. When she is called to jury duty, she generously allows me to have her class for a week. The novel they will be reading has already been selected, since a visit from the author, who lives in Minneapolis, had been scheduled previously.

Never one to teach only the canon, Carolyn had introduced her students to a variety of literature, mixing some predictable AP or college-bound choices with more surprising ones. They have read *As I Lay Dying, Beloved, Stones from the River,* and now this, *Running Fiercely Toward a High Thin Sound,* a first novel about a Jewish family that is divided by the mental illness of one sister and the jealousy of the mother. Mental illness, family dysfunction, lesbian relationships, and Jewish family history and values are all salient themes of the book, which is set in New England in the mid-1970s. Its uniqueness of theme, form, and content make the discussion of this novel particularly suitable for a reader-response approach, since students are bound to have visceral and highly individualistic reactions to the novel.

While Carolyn's taste in literature is contemporary and unconventional, her pedagogy is a bit more traditional and highly effective. The class itself generally focused on some of the more traditional forms of literary analysis that students would be expected to use on the year-end advanced placement exam. The class had been introduced briefly to reader response by a student teacher, but the students seemed to prefer a more text-centered, teacher-led approach to literature. To deepen their collective repertoire of ways of interacting with literary texts, I decided to spend my week with the students using a reader-centered approach.

We began by reviewing some of the basic tenets of reader response with a handout (see Figure 3.2) adapted from an article by Lee Galda (1983). Then I introduced the transactional diagram described in the previous section, very slightly adapted for the novel (see Appendix, Activity 5). I asked the students to fill the diagram out at home and to bring a completed diagram to class the next day. I then asked them to write some "meaning statements" on the back of the handout—one or two sentences that described the meanings they constructed as a result of the transaction between themselves and the text.

We discussed the reader diagrams the following day. Under the reader heading, students listed the following *reader characteristics* (or lack of characteristics) that they felt were important to their reading of the novel:

I have a pushy mommy.

My family has communication problems.

My mom loves me.

What is reader response?

"A reader makes a poem as he reads. He does not seek an unalterable meaning that lies within the text. He creates meaning from the confrontation" (Louise Rosenblatt).

Philosophy or rationale

Reader-response advocates stress the interaction between the reader and the text. Reading is recognized as a process in which expectations operate to propel the reader through the text. Readers bring to the text their own experiences, morals, social codes, and views of the world. Because readers bring their meanings to the text, the responses are different. Response-based teaching pays close attention to the reader, respects the reader's responses, and insists that the reader accept responsibility for making sense of personal experiences.

Response to literature: Theory

In *Literature as Exploration*, Rosenblatt (1968) presented her alternative to the belief that a text carries a precise meaning that readers must try to discern. She proposed that a literary text was simply symbols on a page and that the literary work, or "poem," as she later designated it, existed only in the interaction of reader and text. She defined the literary experience as a "synthesis of what the reader already knows and feels and desires with what the literary text offers" (p. 272). This transaction between reader and text consists of a reader's infusion of meaning into verbal symbols on a page and the text's channeling of that meaning through its construction.

The realization of a literary work of art requires an active reader who constantly builds and synthesizes meaning, paying attention to the referents of the words being processed while aware of the images and emotions experienced. The text does not embody meaning but rather guides the active creation of meaning. Thus, within this theory, it becomes impossible to discuss literature without reference to the reader.

Figure 3.2 Reader Response. *Source:* Adapted from Galda (1983).

My father is not always present in my life.

I have friends who are gay; I know lesbians, how they live and what they are like.

My brother calls me crazy.

I am morally opposed to homosexuality.

I smoke a lot of weed.

I see things in black and white.

I go to a seder every year.

I feel completely exasperated and helpless with my mother.

I am not Jewish.

I am a heterosexual.

I've always wanted to go into a different world.

I am a lesbian.

I am bisexual.

I am an introvert.

I'm obsessive compulsive and know a lot about pot and depression.

I don't like reading about any kind of sex.

I'm mentally unstable.

Nobody close to me has ever died.

I don't usually enjoy reading a book that's totally about somebody else's problem.

Interestingly, on the diagrams most students seemed to focus more directly on what they were not than on what they were, a case of negative identity. I wondered whether this would have been true with any text or whether the students were particularly interested in disassociating themselves from being Jewish or lesbian.

The following *textual characteristics* were offered most commonly:

The book contains a lot of Yiddish words.

Explicit and graphic lesbian sex.

Going through mirrors, a surrealistic quality to the prose.

How the book changes from very realistic to very unrealistic.

Set in an era before my birth, but not forever ago.

So much sex.

All the stereotype of the radical lesbians.

Short chapter.

Magical worlds.

Multiple narratives or perspectives.

After the students listed both the reader traits and the textual characteristics, they were asked to compose several meaning statements that arose from their "unique transactions" with *Running Fiercely Toward a High Thin Sound*. The following *meaning statements* were impressive in their range as well as their gravity:

Books don't have to have redeeming, happy endings because a lot of lives don't.

Sometimes what you perceive is not always the truth.

Families are meshed, there is no changing part of them.

It's important to find the balance between fulfilling your needs and the needs of people close to you.

Mothers do not innately love their children. Society only thinks they should.

Homosexuality is real and important but it is not the book's most important theme.

You can't force your children to be what you want.

Forgiveness is not always possible.

People are often blind to each other's points of view

You should never become so self-centered that you forget you're not the center of the universe.

Accepting other people for who they are instead of what you want them to be is important in family relations.

Silence is dangerous.

I got nothing from this book, it made me feel as if I was reading some sleazy romance novel.

The best route to self-knowledge and enlightenment is to say, "To hell with all of you. I'm going out and doing something that matters! And the easiest road to misery is to vie for power in one's family."

The thing I got out of this book is the concept of love and cruelty, how you really have to love someone before you can hate them or truly be cruel to them.

I found little meaning in this book at all as it didn't apply to me.

CONTRAST OF TWO READERS

What then happens in the reading of a literary work? Through the medium of words, the text brings into the reader's consciousness certain concepts, certain sensuous experiences, certain images of things, people, actions,

scenes. The special meanings and, more particularly, the submerged associations that these words and images have for the individual reader will largely determine what it communicates to him. The reader brings to the work personality traits, memories of past events, present needs, and preoccupations, a particular mood of the moment, and a particular physical condition. These and many other elements in a never-to-be-duplicated combination determine his response to the peculiar contribution of the text.

—Louise Rosenblatt, *Literature as Exploration*

If we are to give credence to this aspect of Rosenblatt's account of what happens in the reading of a literary work, which many of us have, we would expect that the individual characteristics of students would really come into play as they read a novel like *Running Fiercely,* one that is so clearly marked by definitive personal qualities, unusual lifestyles, and unique family history. We might, for example, expect students to have a wide range of responses to such an unusual text, given the diversity of the class. In addition, we might expect students whose "personality traits, memories of past events, present needs, and preoccupations" bear some resonance and similarity to the characters and events of the text to have a markedly different response from those students whose life experiences and memories stand in stark contrast to those that are represented in the novel. The student-response diagrams seem to call these assumptions into question. Although the text is not at all obviously theme-driven, many students seem to have similar transactions with the text, not at all like the never-to-be-duplicated combination that Rosenblatt predicted. While most of the students enjoyed the book, two students seemed unable to make meaning of or to have a positive transaction with the text. Of course, it is not particularly surprising that some students failed to respond to the book; as English teachers, we know that happens all the time. What is surprising, however, is how different these two students are. Their personal qualities are almost diametrically opposed and yet they experienced a similar response to the novel. Their shared resistance seems to call into question some of our assumptions about the relationship between personal qualities and their relevance in terms of how they might influence our responses to a literary text.

Mark

Mark is perhaps the most recalcitrant student in Carolyn's class. He is intelligent and competent, if somewhat surly. His relatively passive and unemotional air didn't seem to waver during the reading of the text, even when the author herself came to visit our classroom in all her radical lesbian splendor.

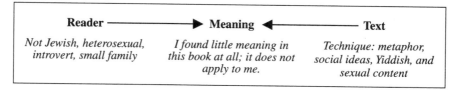

Figure 3.3 Mark's Reader-Response Diagram

Like many of his classmates, Mark listed the relevant reader characteristics in the negative. As a reader he described himself: "not Jewish, heterosexual, introvert, small family." In terms of the textual features that would influence his response, he mentioned: "technique: metaphor, social ideas, Yiddish, and sexual content." See Figure 3.3.

Mark speculated that the novel might be about what he called the "inevitable conflicts between introverts and extroverts" and acknowledged the possibility that the author was telling a metaphorical story that meant something to her, that she was trying to educate the reader about an issue. Yet, in the end Mark came up relatively empty-handed in his transaction: "I found little meaning in this book at all; it does not apply to me."

It would be easy to dismiss Mark's inability to find meaning in this text as having something to do with how different he is from the characters in the book and his difficulty in relating to them. But Mark's classmate Ellen's reaction to the same text cautions us against such a simplistic, if superficially sensible, explanation.

Ellen

Unlike all of her classmates, Ellen is Jewish and speaks Yiddish. Further, she believes that her parents are very much like the selfish, jealous, and woefully imperfect parents of the protagonist. Ellen doesn't find the family dynamics of the novel strange; she recognizes them as being very much like her own. Ellen claims that the mother is bitter, jealous, and mentally unstable. One might think that Ellen's shared characteristics with the characters and situations would make the text especially relevant for her. At the very least, we

might expect that her response would be significantly different from that of a classmate who was as dissimilar from the characters as she was similar. This is not the case.

As did her classmate Mark, Ellen seems to have an unfulfilling transaction with the text (see Figure 3.4). Like Mark, she dismisses the author's motive as being more writer-based than reader-based: "I think Judith Katz wrote this as therapy. I could tell it was based strongly on her life. She wanted to pull out everything that pissed her off and write about it." Ellen fails to map her own experiences onto the text and instead concludes, "I don't think there is a good meaning for this book," a response remarkably similar to Mark's. It may, in fact, be the first thing they have had in common.

The contrast between these two students helps make two points about the use of reader-centered pedagogy in the classroom. I am not suggesting that Rosenblatt argued that students would map their own personal qualities onto the text and that the better the match, the stronger the response would be. For the record, she never claimed anything like that. Our individual qualities, she claimed, would inform our responses to a text but would not necessarily dictate what they were. In practice, though, we have tended to select texts that in provocative ways provide matches between our students' world and the worlds of the characters. While in many ways it may be fruitful to do this, it also may be dangerous, which this contrast points out. First, we may misinterpret how a student's shared experiences and characteristics with those of the characters may affect the student's response. In some ways, as Ellen's case illustrates, the closer the students' own experiences are to the text, the more likely they may be to reject the text. For example, adolescents dealing with suicide attempts of friends or family members might find *Ordinary People* too excruciatingly close to home to read. Second, we inadvertently may be giving students a dangerous message: If you can't "relate" to the book, you may not be able to find meaning in it, or, as Mark so succinctly claimed: "I found little meaning in this book; it doesn't apply to me."

In *Authorizing Readers,* Smith and Rabinowitz (1998) address some of the issues that arise in what they call "the pedagogy of personal experience" (p. 119). They claim that an emphasis on the personality of the reader, which is at the heart of many reader-centered theories and pedagogies, may cause students to ignore diversity and respect for difference. Ironically, developing awareness of differences is one of the goals of our attempt to diversify the curriculum.

We also trivialize some of the profound and perhaps irreconcilable differences between us. As Smith points out, we may be able to appreciate a character's situation but we never will be able to fully understand it. We reduce the power of literature and the representations of those experiences by pretending that we can. Smith claims that the pedagogy of personal response

Reader (Ellen) ————→	**Meaning** ◄————	**Text** (*Running Fiercely*)
(What personal qualities, or events relevant to this particular book, might influence my response?)	*I don't know that there is a good meaning for this book. I think Judith Katz wrote this as therapy. I could tell it was based strongly on her life. She wanted to pull out everything that pissed her off and write about it—the stereotype lesbians, the good girls, and the crazy ones. Some people shouldn't have kids, just because they can get pregnant. Having kids doesn't void you of jealousy. Books don't have to have redeeming, happy endings because a lot of lives don't. Not all mothers are good. Almost any nutcase can get pregnant. A smart person would give that some thought.*	(What textual features might influence my response?)
I'm Jewish, know Yiddish. My mother is bitter and jealous. I'm mentally unstable.		*Yiddish and Jewish references. Fay is just like my mom. They ALL are.*

Figure 3.4 Ellen's Reader-Response Diagram

can make it difficult for students to realize that one doesn't necessarily have to be able to relate to a character to respond to a literary text. He believes it is unrealistic to expect the paths of our lives to map meaningfully onto the lives of characters. Our pedagogy of personal response, he claims, limits students' ability to derive meaning from texts that describe worlds and experiences far different from their own, a reason, ironically, why many of us began to love literature in the first place. Smith quotes a student who feels she cannot respond to Toni Morrison's *Beloved:* "I felt alienated by how their family interacted. I had no basis on which to relate or empathize." Smith agrees that perhaps Toni Morrison is counting on exactly this to make her point—that you can never understand, and that's exactly a part of what you need to understand. This point is especially important in the next section, as we consider the responses of a different literature class to Richard Wright's *Native Son.*

READER RESPONSE AND *NATIVE SON*

Unlike Carolyn's classroom, Martha's twelfth-grade English class is located in a suburb, filled with white-collar families and three-car garages. As part of her advanced placement curriculum, Martha has introduced her students to critical theory. They have read a variety of works, both canonical and nontraditional, including *Beowulf, Much Ado About Nothing, The Things They Carried, Hamlet, Frankenstein,* and *Snow Falling on Cedars.*

Martha's students are familiar with the term *reader response.* In fact, they have completed the "Mushroom" activity and discussed some of the factors that influence their responses to particular texts. They also seem to understand that there are several approaches to a literary text, of which reader response is just one. On the other hand, they have a tendency to oversimplify the concept of reader response as simply meaning: What does this book mean *to me*? That is, they conflate the concepts of personal meaning with the identification of personal characteristics that may affect their responses. They need to clarify their understanding.

Martha has decided to teach Richard Wright's *Native Son* and wants to approach the novel through a variety of critical lenses—Marxist (a natural for this novel), feminist, and reader response. Martha also hopes that the distance between her mostly White, mostly middle-class students and the novel's African American and sometimes violent protagonist Bigger Thomas will help her students see that literary responses are not dependent on one's similarity to a character. She believes, as Smith and Rabinowitz argued, that, in fact, the differences are sometimes precisely the point.

Martha and her students spend about 2 weeks discussing various aspects

of the novel. Then she divides the class into four groups and has them complete an activity called Theory Relay (see Appendix, Activity 6), where they visit a reader-response station, a historical/biographical station, a feminist station, and a Marxist station. The students are asked to describe how each of the four theoretical perspectives informs their understanding of *Native Son*. Each station includes some supporting documents such as biographical information on Richard Wright, explications of Marxist and feminist literary theory (see Chapters 4 and 5), and some quotations from the text that are particularly relevant to each theoretical perspective. Students move around the room from station to station as they listen to the blues.

When students arrive at the reader-response station, there is a description of reader response and a reader-response diagram tailored for *Native Son* (see Appendix, Activity 7). As did Carolyn's class, the students first listed what relevant reader characteristics came into play as they read the text. They then listed the textual characteristics that influenced their responses to the text. Finally, they listed the meaning statements that they derived from their reading transactions. Here is how Martha's students characterized those transactions with *Native Son* from the perspective of reader response.

Reader Characteristics

I'm female.

I'm White.

I'm educated.

I live in the 90s, not the 30s.

My religious background tells me that killing is wrong.

I think the death penalty should be applied in some circumstances.

I've never been told that I can't do what I want to do.

Middle-class suburban home.

Colombian mother.

A history class and my personal experience has taught me about hatred and oppression.

I haven't had to work in order to survive.

The fact that I alone am quite poor.

I am more liberal than the Whites in the novel but less exposed to the ideas of the novel than currently living Blacks.

I have strong views on justice and on taking responsibility for your actions.

I don't believe in the death penalty.

I obviously find myself in a difficult position, unable to help feeling a bit guilty for Bigger's plight and struggles because I am White.

Because I am White, the book was hard for me to relate with. Another large factor is my faith and belief, because I am not a communist it was hard to relate to Jan and Max. Other factors would be *my* society. I don't have the same situation.

I've seen racism happen.

Knowing about history and the civil rights movement gave me a sense both about how far things have come and yet how similar some things still are.

The fact that I am White means that I'll never be able to understand exactly how they felt but I can do my best to stop any oppressive thoughts I may have.

I find myself to be very open-minded. I do try to understand other people's positions. I don't see myself as being prejudicial so I can see both the Black fear and the communist positions well.

I've been oppressed myself in life.

My being against racism would have an effect because that would make me feel a different way about it, the fact that only women are murdered would have an effect as well. I seem to be very sympathetic to remorseful criminals.

I would definitely say that I am like the Bigger who took action. I agree with his desire to want to be in control of his life. I wouldn't murder, yet was it the only way he saw that he could control his life—because I go to the fullest extent in mine. Also so many times in the last 2 years I have wanted to grasp life but it felt so far away. It's really hard to explain or try to live a situation that confuses myself.

Given my personality and my environment, I can't really relate to the feelings Bigger has of fear and oppression. It doesn't really feel he has many options in life (the Whites restrict him) and I am at a point in my life, with high school ending, where I have many options.

I know that it is wrong, but sometimes I am racist and sometimes others are racist against me. I was picked on by a group of Black girls when I was in sixth grade.

I value intelligence.

I am Black in America.

I'm reading the book in class full of White students with a White teacher.

This book is very hard for someone like me to relate to because I don't know what it is like to live in the 1940s. I don't know what it is like to live in poverty. I don't understand Bigger. I look at him and I think, get off your butt and get a job. I understand the oppression but I think there are certain ways he could have escaped from it.

Text Characteristics

Since the story is told from Bigger's point of view, it's biased.

The author is biased about how Blacks were treated because as a Black he has experienced injustice and he also was a communist at the time that he wrote this book.

The closing statements put closure on the story, which made me feel differently about the story.

Persuasive arguments by prosecution and defense.

The preachy nature of the lawyers seem overdrawn and I lose interest.

The extremity of the author's attitude.

The time the story takes place.

The rape—I hate Bigger.

Vivid descriptions.

The way the book is set up from the beginning of White vs. Black.

How gory Mary and Bessie's deaths were.

Max's conversations with Bigger; with Bigger's thoughts that I could actually feel sorry for him.

African American characters; I don't completely understand their conditions.

The Whites in the book don't believe that Blacks are human.

Bigger's brutality inherent in everything he does.

The use of communism makes it difficult to relate with the "good guys."

The descriptive nature in which the author describes the murders and the racist treatment of the Black people; the detailed arguments of the lawyer, who try to give reasons for why things are the way they are also influences my response.

My response to this book has been swayed by racism on both sides. Everyone is blaming everyone else and it affects me. I feel that I am being blamed and I have done nothing to enrage anyone.

The use of three main colors red, white, and black used over and over and over.

Growing up in the 1990s most kids are taught to have respect for all races, and people try to be politically correct so reading the closing statements from the prosecutor and just that whole side of the case is really appalling, especially when Bigger is referred to as a beast and other things, which flat-out classify him as not being human simply because he is Black—not even because he killed two women—I was quite shocked.

Max's ideas and motivation to point out the truth and/or presence of racism took away some of the brutality of the murders. It's harder to think about the murders after Max's statement and the confinement of the African American people.

Meaning Statements

Even with oppression, free will can exist.

If society doesn't treat everyone with the same amount of respect, those lacking respect will rise up against society.

There will always be the resistant or rebellious element in human beings as long as they are oppressed.

Bigger's fear of Whites is what causes him to commit murder.

Although I see the injustice, I can't know what Bigger is feeling because I am not a minority.

I am not a communist so I feel no sympathy for Jan and Max's views. Because of my Whiteness I feel more pain for the White society and don't understand the Black plight. Because of my middle-class status I have no idea of the poverty that Bigger has suffered so I don't feel it as much.

Because I am a White female, Mary Dalton's case is just as tragic as Bigger's if not more so because of her brutal death without any responsibility. Because I am educated Bigger Thomas owes much of his demise to his lack of education and could have done something, if only a bit, about this. Prejudice: Bigger Thomas was under tremendous emotional stress because he was targeted on the basis of his race alone and we should all sympathize with him.

Bigger represents the combination of external and the internal conflicts that Blacks endured because of societal and historical pressures of enslavement.

Bigger could not control his future or fate so he ventured to control instinct, but in the end only a belief system that transcended his doom could save him.

The murder of Mary Dalton and Bessie were symbolic. The former represented the oppressor's voice of misguided goodwill and condescension, and the latter stood for Blacks' willing to be down, subservient, and surrender their spirit.

I'm White so I felt guilty reading about the treatment of Blacks in this book.

This book was not relevant to us.

One's White middle-class background makes it hard to relate to the text.

When things go wrong with Bigger, it hurts me too.

Social and economic pressures are ultimately destructive forces in society.

Society seeks a scapegoat, an opportunity to vent the frustration and hatred, and often puts these feelings in a single incident.

Native Son is about the inability of Whites and Blacks to understand each other.

Sometimes the actions of an individual are controlled by the society he lives in.

I don't think of myself as a prejudiced person, but from reading this I think there is some prejudice in all of us.

My feelings seem to [be] mixed up a bit [about] this story. On one hand I feel bad for Bigger because of his position but I despise someone who could do such a thing.

I feel Bigger Thomas was made into who he is by his society.

As White females it is hard to relate to Bigger; we relate to Mary instead.

I don't understand how Bigger could commit this crime because I was taught to think before I act. His intelligence level was way low.

The racism in this book seemed so unfair to me because I have never really known racism.

I find it hard to relate to Bigger and what he felt because I am a White woman living in a different time period. His feelings and thoughts aren't real to me.

Racism used to be much worse in society than it is now. Segregation is no longer legal, but people still segregate themselves.

The sadness I feel when I am studying the Holocaust indirectly relates to the feelings that Bigger expresses in the book.

Being female I understand the discrimination Bigger faced every day and sympathize with his feelings of rage and helplessness.

DISCUSSION

The reader-response diagrams helped Martha's students isolate the features of the text as well as the personal characteristics that influenced their responses to *Native Son*. As we might expect, many of those responses clustered around issues of race, gender, and class (no wonder some of them invoked the O. J. Simpson trial). Students thought about not only their own race but their own feelings about race relations. They also confronted the intersection between race and gender. White females in particular felt torn between their sympathy for Bigger as an oppressed person and their disgust for his violence. Violence also affected students' responses in terms of their feelings about the death penalty as well as in terms of their visceral reaction to the violence in the story. The reader-response diagrams forced students to think explicitly about the mechanics of their responses and to map those factors in terms

of what belonged to them and what belonged to the text. They made their transactions explicit to themselves, to their teacher, and to their classmates.

Sometimes, completing the diagram forced them to confront the degree to which they were unable or unwilling to have an emotional reaction to the book. For example, one student wrote: "My response as a whole has been quite unemotional. I read Wright's work with interest, see his points, and it raises interesting questions, but I am quite uninvolved, probably largely as a result of my boredom with my life, especially school, and a number of distractions in my mind."

Under the reader characteristics, she wrote: "As a young White middle-class female, I feel I am perhaps better furnished to sympathize with Mary than with Bigger. It is difficult to truly understand the factors in a life leading to such an end, as such pressures and oppression have happily been completely absent from my life." Under the text characteristics, she wrote: "The brutalities Bigger commits are atrocious and while Wright succeeds in explaining Bigger's condition, it does not justify Bigger's actions. Wright intentionally makes his book confusing and therefore disturbing, raising questions about the collective versus the individual in racial issues."

The reader-response station helped to make the mechanics of the reader response explicit and helped students locate the sources of the factors that contributed to their responses. Many students were able to empathize with Bigger despite the profound differences they named between their situations and Bigger Thomas's. Others, like Mark in Carolyn's class and the student quoted in Smith and Rabinowitz (1998), were unable to construct meaning because the text bore no relevance (or so they thought) to their protected and privileged, suburban middle-class lives. Hence, the frequency of meaning statements such as: "This book was not relevant to us." "One's White, middle-class background makes it hard to relate to the text." "This is obviously very difficult for me to personally relate to."

This dismissal because of difference is often where a reader-centered discussion ends: The text was not relevant to me; therefore, I found no meaning in it. As Smith (Smith & Rabinowitz, 1998) points out, this is the inherent irony and limitation in a pedagogy of personal experience, especially when we read multicultural literature or other texts that portray worlds far different from our students'. Martha's students could not simply come up empty-handed because of an unsatisfying personal transaction with the text. Because their reader-response exercise was situated within a multiple perspective approach, they were invited to find meaning in other ways.

In addition, the fact that reader-response was part of a multiple-theory relay allowed students to critique the relative usefulness of the reader-response lens. Martha asked her students to compare and evaluate the four theoretical approaches. She then asked which lens seemed to be most consis-

tent with the intention of the novel, which lens was the most difficult to apply, and which lens was the most informative. Not surprisingly, most students found the Marxist lens among the easiest to apply or the lens that seemed most consistent with the intention of the novel. Most students found it particularly difficult to apply the feminist lens.

While there was some general agreement about the relative usefulness of these two lenses in terms of *Native Son,* the students seemed much more divided about the usefulness of the reader-response lens, with some students reporting that it was the hardest lens to apply and others reporting that it was the most applicable.

DIFFICULTIES STUDENTS REPORTED AS THEY APPLIED THE READER-RESPONSE LENS TO *NATIVE SON*

I'm so used to having to write great statements of theme that when I was presented with an opportunity to simply state my opinions on meaning, I had great difficulty.

The lens that was most difficult to apply for me was the reader-response lens because I questioned what exactly I brought to the text. My experiences with African Americans have been few and far between in terms of person-to-person contact. I'm not consciously racist, but I wonder if I would be more afraid of a Black man walking toward me down a dark Minneapolis alley than a White man. And that makes me feel hypocritical. Because I came in with some mixed feelings about my inner psyche, I wasn't sure how to deal with the reader-response lens.

The reader response was the most difficult. We were reluctant to express our ideas. It does not help that the worksheet wanted us to find meaning through ourselves. I found that it was not possible to find brand new meaning, only twisting of original meaning.

One lens I found surprisingly hard to relate to was reader response. I feel like I haven't had enough experiences with oppression or racism to relate at all to this book. I can't relate to Bigger's feelings because I live in a world that has never limited my options . . . also the feelings of hate the Whites have for Bigger is incomprehensible for me. This is the first time reader response has ever been a difficult lens. It did, however, help me to look at the book in a new light.

SUCCESSES STUDENTS REPORTED AS THEY APPLIED THE READER-RESPONSE LENS TO *NATIVE SON*

I think the reader-response lens went along with the book the best. When we had to fill the reader-response sheet, it helped me see how things in my life related to the book. For me, realizing that the connection between how I was reading the book and being a woman affected each other was huge. I think Wright wanted change and the best way to get that is to be able to relate to others. Reader response helps us do that.

The reader response seemed to be the most attractive to the text. I liked it because it was open-ended and I can use it to interpret *Native Son* as I wanted to.

The reader-response lens seems to be the most consistent with the intention of the novel. Richard Wright is a Black man who writes about Blacks' points of view for White people. The Blacks already know what he is trying to say; it is the White people he is trying to make an impact on. He wants his White audience to think about their own lives and do the best they can to try to relate to the Blacks.

It seems that with the novel, as with any work of art, the artist (author) is most interested in the individual affect each reader experiences. Hence, it seems logical that the lens most consistent with Wright's intention would be reader response, gauging what one has personally gained from reading the novel.

After reading *Native Son*, our group decided that the reader-response lens was the most consistent with the intention of the novel. Depending on your own personal background and views on race and equality, your opinion of the book could be completely different. For example, in the O. J. Simpson case the Blacks thought that it was just another example of police brutality against Blacks and how Blacks are the scapegoats for everything and that this is just another example of their oppression. Whites seemed to think that O. J. Simpson was guilty and that he should be punished. Depending on your race, you can view something totally differently, especially when it has to do with race, like in *Native Son.*

TOWARD A SOLUTION: MULTIPLE VISIONS AND THE NAMING OF PARTS

The reader-response movement was a friendly antidote to the tyranny of the text that characterized some of our earlier approaches to the teaching of

literature. It provided students with a way to engage personally with literature, opened up the possibility of multiple interpretations of individual texts, and made our students the readers—the central element of meaning making with texts. In fact, to some the reader actually became more important than the author. But when reader response becomes not just *a* way of reading, but *the* way of reading texts, it is an ideology, regardless of how appealing that ideology might be. We need to challenge the overly simplistic notion of the individual that has characterized our "pedagogy of personal experience." As I have argued in this chapter, we can do this by directly teaching the elements of reader response.

Martha's and Carolyn's classes demonstrated the value of making our reader-response teaching more explicit. In addition, we've seen that by recontextualizing reader response within a multiple-theory framework, we can create a critical and comparative context that can help us use what is best about the lens of reader response and, at the same time, guard against its excesses by not having it be the only way we encourage students to respond to texts.

Martha's students did indeed consider their reading of *Native Son* from a reader-response perspective, but they did so as they concurrently considered three other theoretical perspectives as well—Marxism, feminism, and biographical/historical criticism. The students considered the viability of those other perspectives as well as their relative effectiveness in helping them make sense of the text. This multiple-theory or comparative perspective can help keep our practice from veering into dogma. The next two chapters deal with Marxism and feminism and how they can contribute to the larger systems that are at play as we read texts and learn to interpret our world through critical encounters.

SUGGESTED ADDITIONAL READINGS

Beach, R. (1993). *A teacher's introduction to reader-response theories.* Urbana, IL: National Council of Teachers of English.
> This volume addresses a variety of critical literary theories that focus on the response of the reader to the text. Theories of response that are discussed include textual, experiential, social, and cultural. The author also has included a chapter on applying theory to practice and making decisions about eliciting student responses in the classroom. A glossary and extensive bibliography are included.

Farrell, E., & Squire, J. (1990). *Transactions with literature: A fifty-year perspective.* Urbana, IL: National Council of Teachers of English.
> Farrell and Squire have put together a collection of essays that underscore the enduring importance of Louise Rosenblatt's *Literature as Exploration.* The book

includes an annotated bibliography provided by the Center for the Learning and Teaching of Literature.

Karolides, N. J. (Ed.). (2000). *Reader response in secondary and college classrooms* (2nd ed.). Mahwah, NJ: Erlbaum.

This greatly expanded second edition is a very useful and readable collection of articles from a wide range of teachers and researchers. Some essays focus on the teaching of specific literary works and offer the teacher specific strategies for implementing reader-response pedagogy. A glossary and a reference section are included.

Nelms, B. (Ed.). (1988). *Literature in the classroom: Readers, texts, and contexts.* Urbana, IL: National Council of Teachers of English.

This book is an older volume planned by the NCTE Yearbook Committee. The subject of this dated but still useful volume is to reassert the central purpose of literature in the English curriculum. The book presents examples of varied response-based approaches to the teaching of literature in elementary and secondary schools.

Probst, R. (1988). *Response and analysis: Teaching literature in junior and senior high school.* Portsmouth, NH: Boynton/Cook.

In this widely used work, the author provides the teacher with suggestions for encouraging students to respond to texts. Probst elegantly and persuasively illustrates the usefulness of the work of Louise Rosenblatt for secondary teachers of literature.

Tompkins, J. (Ed.). (1980). *Reader-response criticism: From formalism to post-structuralism.* Baltimore: Johns Hopkins University Press.

Tompkins has collected a series of essays, which chronologically show the development of discourse around the broad conceptual critical literary position called reader response. The essays discuss the problem of determining the meaning of reader response and are drawn from New Criticism, structuralism, stylistics, phenomenology, psychoanalytic criticism, and poststructuralist theory.

Of Grave Diggers and Kings:
Reading Literature Through the Marxist Lens,
or, What's Class Got to Do with It?

It is *not* that we shouldn't care about individual students and texts. We should, and I do. We also recognize, however, that students and texts are embedded in huge, living, sometimes contradictory networks, and if we want students to understand the workings of textuality, then we have to think about those larger systems.

—Bruce Pirie, *Reshaping High School English*

There is, in fact, no need to drag politics into literary theory: as with South African sport, it has been there from the beginning. I mean by the political no more than the way we organize our social life together and the power relations which this involves.

—Terry Eagleton, *Literary Theory*

The Philosophers have only interpreted the world in various ways; the point is to change it.

—Karl Marx

WHILE THE STUDY of literature in the secondary schools has shuttled somewhat uneasily between text-centered and reader-centered approaches (Applebee, 1993), cultural studies and political approaches to the teaching of literature have moved through our profession like a brush fire. At many colleges and universities, the inclusion of cultural and political lenses such as Marxism and feminism has become the rule rather than the exception. In fact, some have been left to wonder whether the subject of English as we have known it is actually dead and we shouldn't rename our enterprise something like cultural studies (Boomer, 1988; Pirie, 1997).

Critical theory in college-level literary studies has become something of a lightning rod, a conduit of contention about our goals, purposes, and methods of teaching literature (Graff, 1992, 1995; Slevin & Young, 1995). For some, critical theory has energized a once staid and quaint field on the verge of becoming anachronistic. For others, the Marxist and feminist lenses, as well as emphasis on other kinds of cultural criticism and postmodern theories, have drawn us away from what they believe should be at the center of our study—Great Books—and into a morass of subjectivity, relativity, and political correctness.

While most high school classrooms clearly are far removed from this frenzied state of affairs, a few secondary teachers have begun to consider using Marxist and feminist criticism with the texts they teach. Slowly, yet palpably, more secondary teachers have recognized the potential richness and utility of introducing cultural criticism to their students and encouraging them to view literature through political prisms such as Marxism or feminism. Several new secondary literature textbooks have begun to include chapters on cultural criticism. For example, both Harper & Row and Prentice-Hall have published anthologies that now include critical tables of contents and chapters on literary theory (Guerin, Labor, Morgan, & Willingham, 1992; Guth & Rico, 1996). Additionally, high school teachers have begun, with increasing frequency, to adapt critical materials prepared for college students, such as the Bedford Readers. This series provides commentary on such well-known works as *Heart of Darkness* and *Frankenstein* from a variety of critical perspectives, including psychological criticism, feminism, Marxism, and reader response. It appears that the time may be just right to encourage secondary teachers to integrate political literary theory into their literature instruction.

In some respects, there is a great deal of similarity between the feminist and Marxist lenses—they both are political, they both interrogate textual features with considerations of power and oppression, they both invite us to consider the kinds of prevailing ideologies that help construct the social realities in which we participate (or sometimes become unwitting participants). However, the kinds of questions that undergird those lenses and the texts, activities, and student responses to those lenses differ significantly enough that we will explore them in two separate chapters. Elaine Showalter (1989), while acknowledging some of the natural affinities between feminist criticism and Marxist ideologies, reminds us that "feminist criticism cannot go around forever in men's ill-fitting hand-me-downs, the Annie Hall of English studies" (p. 178). The rest of this chapter, then, focuses primarily on the Marxist lens, although there is some discussion that is relevant to the feminist lens as well.

WHY TEACH MARXIST THEORY NOW?

This is a particularly appropriate moment in the history of literacy education to introduce Marxist literary theory into our classrooms. There are a variety of reasons why this is so, reasons that include our increasingly diverse literary canon as well as the changing nature of our students.

Our evolving canon has caused us to consider the cultural and historical factors inherent in looking at a work of literature. Teachers feel compelled to teach background knowledge, including cultural and historical aspects, especially when dealing with multicultural literature. Faced with new literary and cultural territory, teachers find themselves rethinking their approaches to literary texts (Desai, 1997). For example, they may find themselves considering particular aspects of the political content of the text, the author, and the historical and sociocultural context of the work. They also may find themselves thinking about how their students as readers are situated culturally, politically, and personally in relation to the content of the text (Willis, 1997).

Of course, as new historical critics might assert, one could argue that these careful contextual considerations are relevant for all works of literature. Yet, when teaching multicultural literature, teachers seem to have a more acute need to fill in their own knowledge and provide the context for their students. Many teachers express discomfort or a kind of insecurity that springs from their unfamiliarity with the cultural background of the author, the issues that underlie the text, or even the structure of the narrative itself in cases such as *Beloved* or *Ceremony*. This quest for additional knowledge helps set the stage for cultural criticism or for political lenses such as Marxism and feminism.

In addition to our evolving and more inclusive literary canon, the increasing diversity of our students, even in primarily White suburban school districts, underscores our need to integrate cultural criticism into our literary study. In classrooms across the country, teachers have been called upon to heed the different cultural backgrounds of their students and to anticipate how those differences may come to bear on the reading of the literary texts they choose to teach, whether canonical or multicultural. As we acknowledge the diverse backgrounds and perspectives of the students who will read and discuss literary texts together, we also might acknowledge the need to consider particular issues of race and class deliberately and thoughtfully (Hines, 1997). In *Loose Canons: Notes on the Culture Wars,* Henry Louis Gates, Jr. (1992) argues that race *is* a meaningful category in literary studies and the shaping of critical theory:

> Ours is a late twentieth-century world profoundly fissured by nationality, ethnicity, race, class, and gender. And the only way to transcend those divisions—

to forge, for once, a civic culture that respects both differences and commonalities—is through education that seeks to comprehend the diversity of human culture. (p. xv)

For Gates, of course, that education is both a literary and a theoretical one that challenges the centrality of what he calls "our master's pieces" and urges us to consider "the politics of interpretation" as we encounter literature with our students.

This new knowledge is requisite not only for the reading and interpretation of literary texts but for the development of a kind of classroom community where students begin to understand each other and their perspectives (Hines, 1997). This kind of knowledge extends beyond the personal and anecdotal; it extends beyond the individual into the community. In order for students to be able to understand themselves and each other, they need to be able to contextualize their knowledge in terms larger than themselves; in other words, they need to be able to place their own particular situations and the texts they read into a larger system or set of beliefs. It is for precisely this reason that the particular lens of Marxism can be useful.

WHAT THE MARXIST LENS HELPS US SEE

The Marxist lens offers several approaches for literature instruction. One approach is to consider the political context of the texts themselves. Gerry Graff presents the issue of the political content of texts in *Professing Literature* (1987) as well as in *Beyond the Culture Wars* (1992). He quotes George Orwell: "No book is genuinely free from political bias. The opinion that art should have nothing to do with politics is itself a political attitude" (1992, p. 144). Graff and others argue that politics always has been woven inextricably into our literary tradition; like all art, it provides both a representation of ideology and a way to resist it.

Theory, then, helps us pose those political questions, thus reframing what it is we do when we read literature. Bonnycastle (1996) advocates the use of Marxist literary theory because "it places the study of literature in the context of important social questions" (p. 199). This rationale has long been one aspect of what Applebee (1993) calls our "competing traditions" (p. 3) in the teaching of literature. Engagement in important ideas or social issues clearly has been a goal that has shaped our canon, curriculum, and classroom practice. Political lenses such as Marxism and feminism ask us to interrogate rather than simply acknowledge the texts that constitute our cultural heritage.

Using this perspective, students can consider the issues presented in the

text through the lens of the prevailing ideologies of the author's political and historical context. For example, in reading *Of Mice and Men* or *The Grapes of Wrath,* students might consider the plight of migrant workers, John Steinbeck's motives as muckraker, and even Tom Joad as an emblem of the pursuit of freedom (Greene, 1988). The Marxist lens may make possible such readings as the following:

- "the depiction of the sterility of European bourgeois capitalism in the early twentieth century in T. S. Eliot's 'The Wasteland'" (Bonnycastle, 1996, p. 202)
- the axis (centrality) of class in the worlds portrayed in the novels of Jane Austen or the Brontes
- the plight of African Americans as seen through the eyes of Bigger Thomas in Richard Wright's *Native Son* and Wright's eventual indictment of American society as racist

In addition to examining the political content of texts, Marxist literary theory also encourages students to consider the ways in which literary texts and the reading audiences for those texts—including themselves, their classmates, and their teachers—are socially constructed. As McCormick (1995) argues, using culturally situated theories such as Marxism is important

> so students can see that they, as readers, are socially constructed subjects, that texts are also constructed in particular social contexts—which may be quite different from their own and which they may need to study—and that different ways of telling stories have consequences. (p. 307)

Pirie (1997) also underscores the importance of students' awareness of audience construction and the role that theories such as Marxism and feminism can play in facilitating that awareness:

> For any text we can ask students what kind of ideal audience is being constructed. Who does this story think its readers are? Who would it like them to be? What does it assume about the reader's attitudes, values, and prejudices and about the best ways of trying to change those attitudes? Or is it trying to change the reader at all? We can then compare our responses as actual audiences: Do we willingly allow the text to construct us in the shape of its ideal reader, or do we find ourselves resisting at some points? Should we? Marxist and feminist critics have for some time enacted the possibility of audience resistance by constructing readings that expose and critique the ideologies of canonical works, but this form of reading is still uncommon in high school literature classes. (p. 30)

Mary Beth Hines (1997) quotes a college teacher who uses Marxism and other forms of cultural criticism to promote his pedagogical priorities of social justice: "I want to stress that the text is a social construction and if it's a social construction, then who constructed it, what's it doing, and what are the mechanisms that are at work here?" (p. 129). This notion of construction is a central element of students' ability to learn to read and interpret literature, to read both resonantly (Wolf, 1988) and resistantly.

It is not only the political content of the texts themselves or the ways in which audiences are constructed by those texts that can be read through a Marxist lens; Marxist theory makes visible the idea that literature itself is a part of ideology. Bonnycastle (1996) writes, "A further role of Marxist criticism is that of pointing out and documenting the way in which literature and 'the literary' function as a part of ideology" (p. 203). He claims, "Theory is subsersive because it puts authority in question. . . . It means that no authority can impose a 'truth' on you in a dogmatic way—and if some authority does try, you can challenge that truth in a powerful way, by asking what ideology it is based on" (p. 34).

Selden (1989) explains Eagleton's assertion of the relationship between literature and ideology this way:

> The text may appear to be free in its relation to reality (it can invent characters and situations at will), but it is not free in its use of ideology. Ideology here refers not only to conscious political doctrines but to all those systems of representation which shape the individual's mental picture of lived experience. The meanings and perceptions produced in the text are a reworking of ideology's own working of reality. (p. 42)

McCormick (1995) argues that the use of critical theory can present "reading to students as a deeply imbedded cultural act" (p. 305). In other words, critical theory can help students to question the content of their own education—what is present and what is absent. We can use critical theory to make our canonical choices explicit and potentially debatable for students. As Graff (1992) argues, theory encourages us to teach the conflict or the controversy of our literature curriculum and of the "culture wars" that fuel that curriculum. In response to William Bennett, Henry Louis Gates, Jr. (1992) writes, "The teaching of literature *is* the teaching of values; not inherently, no, but contingently, yes; it is—it has become—the teaching of an aesthetic and political order in which no women or people of color were ever able to discover the reflection or representation of their images, or hear the resonances of their cultural voices" (p. 35, emphasis in original).

Secondary teachers can use Marxist literary theory to help bring into greater visibility the issues of power, class, ideology, and resistance that are

embedded in the texts they read with their students. When paired with canonical texts, the Marxist lens can be especially useful in revitalizing texts that seem tired or anachronistic. This is in part what Graff (1991, 1992) refers to in his now famous argument on "how to save 'Dover Beach'": "I concluded in my *Harper's* essay (1991) that the best way to rescue poems like 'Dover Beach' was not to try to protect them from the critical controversies about their value, but to use those controversies to give them new life" (Graff, 1995, p. 133). Marxist literary theory can help shape that debate, whether it centers on the literary merit of the text itself, on reading the text politically, or on recognizing the text as a cultural construction or part of our overarching ideology.

In the next section a secondary teacher uses the Marxist lens with *Hamlet* to encourage students to consider ideology and social class as they read literary texts.

READING *HAMLET* THROUGH THE MARXIST LENS, OR, "WHY DO THE GRAVEDIGGERS SEEM TO KNOW MORE ABOUT LIFE THAN ANYONE?"

In a suburban classroom, where the student parking lot is filled with cars far nicer than those their teachers can afford to drive, an advanced placement English class is studying *Hamlet*. With few exceptions, the students in this class have lives that are privileged and full of possibilities. Nearly all of these students, sons and daughters of white-collar professionals, will go to college. They think nothing of dropping hundreds of dollars on prom night. They are the envy of the rest of the students in the school: the beautiful people— smart, popular, and affluent. They're basically good people, motivated learners, and engaged students, but they hardly ever think beyond the boundaries of their own comfortable world.

Michael, their teacher, has ambitious goals. He wants to engage his students in great literature. He wants to teach a college-prep English course rigorous enough to help his students sail through the year-end AP test. He wants to help his students create some provocative links between Hamlet's world and their own, links that extend beyond the connections of personal response, as powerful as those responses sometimes might be. Somewhat hesitantly Michael explains, "I've always worked on getting kids to respond to whatever we read on a personal level, to relate to the characters and their situations by thinking of similar situations of their own, to find a way into the text through their own personal experience. But lately I've been thinking, I don't know, more politically. I want my students to think about the worlds these texts both represent and invoke. I want them to think about what set

of beliefs drive these characters and, in some cases, help seal their fate. I want them to think about the author's relationship to those sets of beliefs. I think I sometimes forget to help them see the big picture. And lately, I've been doing all this reading on contemporary criticism and I found myself thinking that these suburban kids never talk about class or privilege, even though or maybe because they're surrounded by it. So, I thought I'd try Marxism with *Hamlet* this time and see what happens."

On a drab winter morning colored only by the bright blue classroom carpeting and a bulletin board full of senior class pictures, Michael begins class by asking his students to consider the role of power in *Hamlet*. "What kinds of power do you see operating in the play?" asks Michael. There is a virtual cacophony of response.

"Power about who rules."

"Power about who's king."

"Power about property."

"Power over other people's lives, like Rosencrantz and Guildenstern."

"Power over whether certain countries go to war and who gets to fight them."

"Personal power. Like Hamlet over Ophelia."

"OK. Let's think about power in a particular way today," says Michael. "Who's got it, who doesn't have it, and why. And, let's think about where power comes from, both now and in Shakespeare's time. I understand that some of you took Russian history with Mr. Murphy last semester. What can you guys tell me about Karl Marx?"

"Father of communism?"

"Power to the Proletariat!"

"What's the Proletariat?"

"Power to the people!"

"Same thing!"

Michael distributes a handout entitled Key Ideas of Marx (see Appendix, Activity 8) and quickly reviews it with the students. In addition to Marx's beliefs about the stages of history and dialectical materialism, the class discusses capitalism, class struggle, working-class misery, and class consciousness. Then Michael says, "In addition to the Marxism we've been talking about, there is also something called Marxist literary theory. Marxist literary theory is a kind of political lens through which we can read works of literature. Marxist literary theory asks us to consider the social structures that are portrayed in a particular work and how power is allocated among different social groups. Many Marxist critics believe that we cannot understand individual people or literary characters or even authors without understanding their social positions and the larger systems in which those social positions operate. Marxist literary theory also asks us to notice in the texts we read

what is the dominant view of the world, a prevailing set of beliefs, or ideologies. What are some ideologies or sets of beliefs that you've come across?"

"Freedom of speech."

"Equality."

"Democracy."

"How the world was created. I think there are a bunch of ideologies about that!"

"Anyone can succeed if they try hard enough."

"That's crap."

Michael smiles and says, "Hmmmm. We'll be getting to that later. Now what seems to be the prevailing ideology or ideologies that operate in the world of *Hamlet*?"

"The divine right of kings," says one student.

"That women are powerless," says another.

"Yeah, they couldn't even play themselves."

"We are born into our lot in life."

"Royalty are better than other people and have the right to rule other people."

"That gravediggers have a much different view of the world from the bottom than Claudius does from the top."

"Great. You bring me to my next question. Aren't we in some way thinking about society as a social ladder, kinda like we do with things here at this school? Take a look at this." Michael then distributes a handout entitled Reading *Hamlet* Through the Marxist Lens (see Appendix, Activity 9). He directs them to a drawing of a "social ladder." Then, after a spirited discussion about the social ladder of their particularly cliquish school, the students consider the social ladder of the play. Michael designed the vertical diagram to demonstrate graphically the existence of hierarchy—something that is important not only in the discussion of Marxism but in laying a conceptual foundation for a discussion of patriarchy, which will come during a discussion of feminist literary theory that Michael has already begun to think about.

Michael next asks his students to consider pairs of characters in terms of who has power and who does not. Michael asks students to indicate which of the sets of power struggles they listed might be considered class conflicts. Michael wants his suburban students to be able to read the text with a heightened awareness of class and privilege—their own and the characters'. He encourages his students to examine the agency of social class in the play as well as in their reading of it. In fact, when asked to consider where they would situate themselves relative to issues of power, the students provide responses that are telling. Michael asks students to place a mark on a concentric circle graph (shown in Activity 9) that indicates where they are in relation

to the center of money and power. There are five concentric rings: One is the closest to the center of power and money, and five is the most distant.

More than 75% of the students place themselves in the second or third circle, closest to the center of money and power. Only a few students place themselves in the fourth or fifth circle, farthest from the center of power. By contrast, one student actually places himself right in the center!

Even though Michael carefully constructed this part of the activity so that students would reflect privately on their own economic status, his usually compliant students seem a bit uncomfortable with this exercise; in fact, some are overtly hostile. "What does our social status have to do with reading *Hamlet?*" asks Tim, an Ayn Rand fan. "Social status isn't that important. People make too much of it. And besides, Marx wasn't born until after Shakespeare died, I mean, like, way after? Marxism wasn't around then. So, how can we use it to read the play?"

Michael isn't quite prepared for this resistance. He finds himself challenged and feels even more strongly about the importance of pursuing this line of inquiry. He asks his students to try to consider how issues of class might have affected their reading of *Hamlet*. He also asks them to consider, "What characters in *Hamlet* do you feel most closely represent where you are socially?"

The student responses are varied. They struggle desperately to discover a Shakespearean middle or upper middle class, one that would mirror their own location. Many students think that characters such as Laertes, Polonius, Horatio, and Ophelia somehow make up that middle class.

I am an average middle-class person. Closest to Ophelia.

Polonius and his family. I guess they were right in the middle.

For the students, the middle class represents people with some resources and power but with a reasonable perspective that neither royalty nor the working class seems to possess. These middle-class characters—Horatio, for example—allow students to understand both groups—those more and those less fortunate than they. It is clear that students feel this is a perspective they have, not only on the characters in the play but on their own lives.

I think being in the middle of things I can be pretty open-minded about the class structure on the whole.

Being in-between having the power and having no power, I am able to sympathize with all groups.

I believe that my position in the circle allows me to see both sides of the coin.

Many students express affinity for Horatio—neither rich nor poor, not quite a commoner, not quite royalty—a sort of Everyman with class.

I can see things more clearly because I am neither rich nor poor. I am probably most like Horatio—he does OK but he isn't royalty.

Horatio seem the most like me. He's in the middle of the ladder but sort of near the top.

I'm like Horatio. Being in the middle, it's easier to be unbiased. I can see both ends of the spectrum—those with money and power and those without.

I think Horatio is in this place too—well-educated and financially stable/well-off. He also has friends in higher classes than himself.

As far as wealth goes, I resent the king for his ignorant abuse of power and manipulation. I feel sorry for the servants and courtiers who had to remain inferior. I would be Horatio or Ophelia, accessible.

I identify with Horatio a great deal. He is involved with the upper class but not because he's vying for a place in circle number one. He focuses on his friends, not on their social and economic worth.

This "Horatio affinity" characterizes the responses of most of the class, in terms of both character identification as well as economic identification. Students seem comfortable marking themselves as being close to power through either money or friends, like Horatio, but not totally within the epicenter of the prevailing power structure, like Hamlet.

While most of this suburban advanced placement class is solidly middle to upper middle class, there are a few students in the class whose social status is quite different from that of their more wealthy classmates. These students marked the fourth or, in one case, fifth circle out from the center of power and seemed eager to claim affinity for a different set of characters as well as to announce their less fortunate economic status.

I have more in common with the lower social characters; root for the underdog.

Probably the lower-class servants. They have to work pretty hard and can't advance right now anyway because of circumstances. I live with

> my mom because my parents were recently divorced and there is no child support coming.

> I guess I would be considered a gravedigger with potential. Economically, I don't live in Sunfish Lake [the wealthiest part of the school district], so my blue-collar family can't compare to royalty.

> I would say that I am a player. The gravediggers are a little too low and I have the potential to get close to power and money; I doubt I could be President, but perhaps I'll work in the White House.

Many students reported that they never had seriously considered issues of class before and didn't feel that issues of power and class affected their reading of *Hamlet*. These students seemed almost offended or apologetic by the suggestion that considerations of power and privilege might have affected their reading.

> If my social status affected my interpretation of *Hamlet* in any way, I honestly was not aware of it.

> I really did not feel like it affected anything.

> When I read *Hamlet*, I did not feel the class struggle applied to me in my life.

In summary, most students reported that issues of power and class clearly affected their response to the play, although they might not have been aware of it as they read. These students crossed all divisions of class—some saying that it affected their reading because they had power, some saying that considerations of status affected their reading precisely because they did not have power, and some indicating they were in that middle "Horatio" position.

One student wrote: "It (my social status) definitely affected my reading. Being somewhat higher than the average individual made me side more with the higher characters. Hamlet represents me well because there aren't any 'rich' people I know . . . so the only people higher are my parents." Another, who like many of her classmates felt most closely aligned economically with Horatio, grudgingly admitted: "My social status may have changed my point of view about certain characters and their status." Similarly, another student responded: "Yes, it made me like Horatio so much more because he didn't have the power."

Other students felt that socioeconomic issues caused them to identify with the lower-status characters.

> It makes me sympathize more with the lower classes.

Yes. I believe that the royal elite are my enemies. I fit most closely with Rosencrantz and Guildenstern.

I feel that living in a family who is friends with people who have power makes me relate to Polonius and especially his children. I know what it feels like to be friends with people who have power and to envy that power even though you are their friends.

I think I saw Guildenstern's view easier because he fits my location. It was easier to see how he felt because he was not at the top.

Many female students felt they related most closely to Ophelia. For them, issues of gender seem to be more salient than issues of class. A few noted the conflation of gender and class. Here are a few illustrative comments:

I identify with Ophelia because she is without much influence but with a fair amount of wealth. She sings lot and is in love with Hamlet, just like me.

I feel closest to Ophelia because although she is high class (because of family, like me), she is a woman and doesn't get much consideration for her own well-being.

I probably feel I am most closely represented by Ophelia. Ophelia is one of the few females in the book and she does not have a lot of power, money, but she's not near the bottom of the social scale.

The character that best represents me is Ophelia. She really didn't care that much about money, only about love.

And, of course, several students unabashedly related most to Hamlet. These students (all male) invariably were self-identified in either the second or, in one case, the first circle of power and privilege.

Hamlet. . . . I understand his confused thought, his limitless potential, and his sometimes depressed outlook.

It may sound egotistical, but it is hard not to identify, at least a little bit, with Hamlet.

Hamlet is the character that I most identify with, since his positions and responsibility force him to distance himself socially.

I *am* Hamlet. I am not going to be king, but how Hamlet thinks and acts I can definitely relate to.

I am most close to Hamlet: Sometimes I feel as though I need to solve problems I didn't create.

THE BIG QUESTIONS

Marxism encourages us to look at big questions, and it has developed impressive tools for doing that. The main use of Marxism in literary studies rests in adapting those methods, especially those dealing with ideology, to help us talk about and resolve the smaller problems, which occupy most of us most of the time.

—Stephen Bonnycastle, *In Search of Authority*

For the most part, Michael felt he had accomplished a good deal by having his students try on the Marxist lens, in however simplistic a version. They discussed the concept of ideology and read the text for evidence of it. They discussed power and class structure in terms of how it affected the characters and the play, and considered the characters not just as individuals but as players in a large social and economic system. Michael also felt that students had, for perhaps the first time, considered their own social status and explored the possibility that their own position in the prevailing social structure might have influenced their reading of the text as well as the level of affinity they felt for any particular character. Finally, Michael felt that reading *Hamlet* through the Marxist lens enabled students to do precisely what Bonnycastle claims Marxism is particularly good at doing—encouraging us to ask both the big and the small questions. On the last question of the Marxist handout (see Appendix, Activity 9), Michael asked his students to think of both large and small questions grounded in the Marxist lens. He encouraged them to think of some questions that were concerned with the world of the text and questions that concerned them on a more personal level. Michael was gratified by the range and depth of questions and by the evidence that they actually had been peering at *Hamlet,* and at themselves, through the Marxist lens. Here are some of their questions:

About the Text

Through a Marxist lens I see that the relationship between Ophelia and Hamlet was deeply rooted in monetary and class struggles. Why that was not evident before is unknown to me.

Is having so much power good for human nature?

If Ophelia was so high up, why was her only point in the story to go crazy?

Do women really have any power—even in the highest classes?

Why does Hamlet feel he can dismiss the lives of Rosencrantz and Guildenstern?

Why is it that the gravediggers seem to know more about life than anyone?

About Themselves

I often wonder if true love can exist anymore, with people so greedy and cynical.

Why can the middle class be fooled so easily by the upper class? Does the upper class have the right to use the underclass like they do? Does social position justify treating someone as if they are inferior?

Are all people in power destined to fall?

Are people powerful mostly by luck?

Does power mean you can do anything, even if it's illegal?

Are all people created equal? Darwinian evolution suggests they are not. By resisting class differences does one destroy human nature?

Why should society be based on rank? Are you a better person because you have power and or money?

As he and his students discussed these questions, Michael knew that the Marxist lens enriched and complicated their reading of *Hamlet* and highlighted some details that otherwise might not have been heeded. He was glad that, in addition to the personal-response strategies and the textual and New Critical strategies they brought into the class with them, they now had Marxist literary theory as part of their interpretive repertoire or tool kit.

CHALLENGES IN PRESENTING MARXIST LITERARY THEORY

Teaching Marxist literary theory in secondary schools is a complicated enterprise. Some students may be resistant to the whole notion of the Marxist lens. As one student wrote in response to the Marxist handout: "I found this question to be offensive and pointless. My perception allows me to imagine

myself at any point in the circle." Or, "The social ladder is an arbitrary construct and I don't choose to think of myself in those terms. Therefore, the question is meaningless." One student wrote, "Thinking about the Marxist ideology makes me realize how Marxism undermines morality. Morality consists in making choices that respect the rights of others. By focusing on class conflict, Marxism obliterates the idea of personal responsibility and implies that any action is justified to help one win the class conflict, and thus no morality is possible."

As Bonnycastle (1996) points out:

> There is an unconscious hostility to some Marxist ideas in most students, especially if they are consciously trying to "improve themselves." One way to measure how you are improving is to see how you are rising on the social scale; and if you feel you have moved yourself up to a new level, that is a clear indication of success. But this measuring stick entails a class system, with many of the unattractive features inherent in such a system, such as competition and the victory of the winner paid for by the suffering of the loser. (p. 200)

It is difficult for all of us, and especially for students, to critique and resist the prevailing ideology as we participate in it. Many of the students in Michael's suburban advanced placement class found the Marxist lens to be alienating and uncomfortable. And yet it was this very discomfort and their obliviousness of their location in educational and economic privilege that contributed to Michael's desire to introduce them to the Marxist lens.

In addition to student resistance, there may be other forms of resistance to critical encounters with Marxist literary theory. Some politically conservative communities may confuse the introduction of Marxist literary theory with the practice or indoctrination of communism, and teachers may receive negative reactions from parents, community members, administrators, and other teachers. Even parents who consider themselves to be open-minded may be confused by the term *Marxist*. Indeed, discussing the differences between Marxism and Marxist literary theory is a difficult but necessary element of introducing students to this critical lens. Those discussions may indeed help diffuse some community resistance. On the other hand, that very resistance may be the strongest proof that we need the vision the Marxist lens provides to read our ideologies and to teach our students of literature to do the same.

Now let us turn to another political prism, the feminist lens. It too encourages us, as Bonnycastle (1996) said, to "look at the big questions," to name and resist ideology, and to "help us talk about and resolve the smaller problems, which occupy most of us most of the time" (p. 205), which in

this case, are the "problems" of gender as they relate to the reading and interpretation of literary texts.

SUGGESTED ADDITIONAL READINGS

Barret, M. (1991). *The politics of truth: From Marx to Foucault.* Stanford: Stanford University Press.
    In this work Barret discusses and critiques classical Marxism and theories of ideology, the collapse of the Marxist model, values of post-Marxism, and a new concept of ideology as another route to socialism.

Baxandall, L., & Morawski, S. (Eds.). (1973). *Marx and Engels on literature and art: A selection of writings.* St. Louis: Telos.
    This volume includes a long and informative introduction by the editors, and important passages from Karl Marx's and Friedrich Engels's works.

Frow, J. (1986). *Marxism and literary history.* New Haven: Yale University Press.
    In this volume, the author examines important works by Eagleton, Jameson, and Macherey. He discusses Marxism and structuralism, discourse and power, Russian formalism and the concept of literary system, literary history, and intertextuality.

Gramsci, A. (1971). *Selections from the prison notebooks* (Q. Hoare & G. N. Smith, Trans. & Eds.). New York: International Press.
    Gramsci's *Prison Notebooks* are considered his most important works. His most significant doctrine for literary studies is the concept of "hegemony." Gramsci is of interest to literary theorists because he rejects shortsighted views that literary works are solely vehicles for political views and reflections of economic conditions.

CHAPTER FIVE

A Lens of One's Own: Of Yellow Wallpaper and Beautiful Little Fools

We don't know what women's vision is. What do women's eyes see? How do they carve, invent, decipher the world? I don't know. I know my own vision, the vision of one woman, but the world seen through the eyes of others? I only know what men's eyes see.

—Viviane Forrester, "What Women's Eyes See"

I have a male mind with male experiences. Therefore I see things through the perception of a man. I couldn't relate to some of Virginia Woolf's view and I despised the way she pushed her view on the reader. This was brought on by my masculinity, I feel.

—Bill, Grade 12, after reading *A Room of One's Own*

Being a feminist is not a gender-specific role.

—Erin, Grade 11

[F]eminist critical theory is a microcosm of the entire theoretical universe, in which a power struggle continues unabated.

—Raman Selden, *A Reader's Guide to Contemporary Literary Theory*

IT'S SECOND HOUR in Jen's twelfth-grade literature class. We've been talking about feminism and have been trying our collective hand at applying "the feminist lens" to everyday life, to things like Madonna's lingerie, Mount Rushmore, and the Miss America pageant (see Appendix, Activity 10). I tell the students about something that happened the other day at the airport. The gate agent made an announcement reminding passengers of the new one-piece-of-carry-on-baggage-per-passenger rule. She clarified that for women the bag may be in addition to a purse, and that for men the bag may be in addition to a computer case or briefcase. I looked down at my own computer

case and shook my head in disbelief. The students listen appreciatively to the anecdote.

We then move to a discussion about the amount of attention the 1998 Olympic women's championship hockey team received compared with the fanfare that greeted the 1984 "Miracle on Ice" hockey team. Ironically, today's class periods are shortened to accommodate a pepfest to send off the women's basketball team to the state tournament. When I ask how many students plan to attend the game, only a handful of students raise their hands. I wonder aloud if more students would be attending the game if it were a men's basketball game. Without hesitation, nearly all the students agree that most of them would indeed attend the finals of the men's basketball game at the state tournament, although, they point out somewhat bitterly, the men's team has never made it that far.

There are two female basketball players in the class, resplendent in their red and gold uniforms (or at least as resplendent as anyone can be in uniforms that are red and gold). They, too, agree that their championship game will be poorly attended, but when pressed, they offer some surprising sympathy for their nonfans.

"Well, it *is* true that our game is different than the guys," offers one of the players.

"Yeah, it's slower, and the rules are harder to understand," concedes the other.

"Yeah," agrees the first. "I guess I can see why not a lot of people want to come to watch us play. We're not that exciting."

"Wait a minute!" comes a cry from the back of the classroom. It's Geoff, who happens to play on the men's basketball team. "You're dissing yourself. Shouldn't we put on that, you know, feminist lens?"

Shouldn't we, indeed?

WHY TEACH FEMINIST THEORY NOW?

Viviane Forrester's (1980) acknowledgment of the dominance of men's vision, or "what men's eyes see," provides an explicit rationale for teaching contemporary feminist literary theory to adolescents. Theory provides us with a way of recognizing and naming other visions while promoting our own ways of seeing. Theory helps us recognize the essential quality of other visions: how they shape and inform the way we read texts, how we respond to others, how we live our lives. Theory makes the invisible visible, the unsaid said.

Theory asks us to treat the text and our responses to it as cultural objects. Rather than removing us farther from the world, feminist theory asks

us to invoke our world as we read, interpret, and evaluate texts. As Eagleton (1983) remarks:

> Literature, we are told, is vitally engaged with the living situations of men and women; it is concrete rather than abstract, displays life in all its rich variousness, and rejects barren conceptual enquiry for the feel and taste of what it is to be alive. (p. 196)

Feminist literary theory invites us to consider a wide variety of issues of gender, of "the living situations" of men and women, as we read. Feminist literary theory asks us to attend to the cultural imprint of patriarchy as we read. We do this by heeding features of language, of canon formation and transformation, of the nuanced voices of female and male writers, and of the portrayal of masculine and feminine experience.

Theory also tries to capture the complexities of human existence as it is portrayed in literary texts. In his recent plea to shift our notion of literary studies to a broader vision of cultural studies, Bruce Pirie (1997) calls for a high school literature program that would "treat texts as constructions within intertextual webs, sponsored by institutions and interacting with audiences and would also encourage a study of our own situation as readers" (p. 97). Political literary theories such as feminism and Marxism require readers to ask questions about the construction of culture, of texts, and of meaning as they seek to construct their own interpretations.

There are, of course, as many "feminisms" as there are "Marxisms," and it is easy for both teachers and students to become confused about feminist theory, or even feminism, for that matter. As Elaine Showalter (1989) writes, "Not even feminist critics seem to agree what it is they mean to profess and defend" (p. 169). Two of the classroom activities I include reflect a working definition of feminism (see Appendix, Activities 11 and 12). In a true feminist tradition, the definition continues to evolve.

As with Marxism, the point of reading with feminist theory, of course, isn't to transform unsuspecting and largely apolitical high school students into feminists (or Marxists); the point is to help adolescent readers read texts and worlds more carefully as they become aware of the ideologies within which both are inscribed. Bonnycastle (1996) writes, "Feminist literary criticism has a political and moral dimension. It doesn't need to be revolutionary, but, like Marxism, it does aim at changing the world and the consciousness of people in the world" (p. 194).

Like the Marxist theories we discussed in Chapter 4, feminist literary theory provides a lens through which students can interpret literature and life. As students read and interpret literary texts, feminist theory can help them to notice salient issues of gender—the portrayal of women in the world

of the novel, the gender of the author and what relevance it may bear to how the work is both written and received, the ways in which the text embraces or confronts prevailing ideologies of how men and women are situated in the "real world," and the ways in which our own interpretations as individual readers are gendered.

WHAT STUDENTS CAN SEE WITH FEMINIST THEORY

There are at least four dimensions in which using feminist theory can transform students' reading—how students view female characters and appraise the author's stance toward those characters, how students evaluate the significance of the gender of the author in terms of its influence on a particular literary work, how students interpret whole texts within a feminist framework, and finally, and perhaps most important, how students read the gendered patterns in the world. To explore how feminist theory can inform the literary experience of adolescents, I developed some activities to use with a variety of literary texts. Working with teachers in both urban and suburban classrooms, I introduced students to the feminist lens and chronicled their attempts to adopt gendered considerations of texts, of authors, of characters, of themselves as readers, and of the world around them. I describe some of these literary transactions below.

WHAT COLOR ARE YOUR WALLS? CHANGING THE WAY WE VIEW FEMALE CHARACTERS

One way the feminist lens can inform how students make meaning of texts is by refocusing their reading of female characters. As some feminist critics assert (Showalter, 1985), readers should learn to recognize what happens to female characters under the "male gaze" of authors. How does the fictional portrayal of female characters reflect the reality of women's lives? How does the creation of female characters reinforce or resist certain social attitudes toward women? And, finally, how are we as readers implicated in what is essentially a gendered act as we read and interpret the lives of women who people the pages of the works of literature we read?

In previous work (Appleman, 1993), I illustrated how students' interpretive vision adapted easily to the lens of feminism as they considered characters from *Of Mice and Men, Ordinary People,* and *The Great Gatsby.* I asked students to make traditional descriptions of these female characters and then to make a different sort of statement in light of our discussion of feminist theory. Here are some examples of the results:

Curley's Wife

TRADITIONAL STATEMENT

She was a bad girl, a tease, and a flirt.

FEMINIST STATEMENT

She's just been treated poorly by her horrible, selfish, chauvinistic husband. She is not bad.

Beth

TRADITIONAL STATEMENT

She's the great American bitch.

FEMINIST STATEMENT

She's a repressed woman who is trapped by society's expectations of what a wife and mother should be.

Daisy

TRADITIONAL STATEMENT

She was a "beautiful little fool" who depended on her husband to take care of her.

FEMINIST STATEMENT

Her husband took control of her and wouldn't let her think for herself. She was doing her best within the limits of women's role in society.

I decided to explore feminist theory with Martha Cosgrove's students, who had just finished reading *Hamlet*. We met Martha in Chapter 3 as she introduced her twelfth-grade students to multiple critical approaches to *Native Son*. (We'll spend even more time with her in Chapter 7.)

As part of our introduction to the feminist lens and of our larger purpose of demonstrating that different classical or canonical texts can be viewed from more than one theoretical perspective, we asked students to read Gertrude and Ophelia through a feminist lens. Note that these students had

already considered *Hamlet* from a Marxist perspective (see Chapter 4). In addition to encouraging multiple perspectives, we also wanted to emphasize the intertextual nature of interpretation. That is, a critical lens is not an artifact of interpretation suitable to only a particular text but rather is a flexible tool that can be used with a variety of texts.

After a brief explication of the feminist lens (see Appendix, Activity 11), we asked students to consider Gertrude and Ophelia from the perspective of the feminist lens and to contrast that with statements using a "traditional" perspective, one that didn't consciously incorporate any considerations of gender into its interpretation. Here are some of the resulting descriptions:

Gertrude

TRADITIONAL STATEMENTS

She is the queen, she has some power.

She is an adequate woman of the times, and she plays her role of loyalty and servitude toward the men in her family.

Gertrude is the queen who lost her husband and immediately married another.

Gertrude is simply the mother of Hamlet and the queen of the country.

Wife of two kings.

She is a queen who lives how she wants to live.

FEMINIST STATEMENTS

She is more of a plot device than of thematic importance herself.

She is a woman who wants control of her life.

Was she so dependent that she had to marry Claudius?

She's defined by her husbands and her son.

Despite the illusion of power, she is actually powerless. She is not allowed to advise on matters of importance but must be advised in all she does. She is not really trusted to take care of herself.

She is robbed by Shakespeare of a character with personality power.

Ophelia

TRADITIONAL STATEMENTS

Sheltered and devoted to those who love her; always tries to please her family while following her heart.

Innocent, typical daughter and sister, who desires Hamlet.

Emotional, young, innocent, weak, fragile; she needs protection.

She is overemotional.

Ophelia was a girl of reasonable status in the kingdom which implanted a daring notion that she may someday marry the prince, Hamlet.

She is a typical young and innocent girl who is caught up in her emotions and troubled by them.

FEMINIST STATEMENTS

Her feelings and identity have been repressed by the male figures in her life. When her father is killed, she is separated from that control and goes crazy with the release of her pent-up identity.

Trapped in her traditional role, she's always being told what to do by a man—her father, her brother, and Hamlet.

Any woman of sound body and mind like Ophelia had, at least to begin with, should have the power and right to pursue life as she pleases without the restraint of society's rules and arranged marriages.

She is forced into insanity by the forces of the men in her life. All of her emotions depend on Hamlet's actions.

Ophelia cannot escape her oppression by men except by insanity and death.

Ophelia subjects herself to "the slings and arrows" of Hamlet as her oppressor, her love.

Ophelia's fears and concerns are dismissed as frivolity because of her gender.

This exercise enabled students to cast two characters they already knew well in the light of a feminist interpretation. They seemed to be able do so

with ease. The contrast of the traditional perspective with the feminist perspective helped underscore some of the more salient features of a feminist interpretation. In addition, it helped students exercise a kind of mental flexibility, one of the goals of the multiple-theory approach to literature advocated by this book. That is, rather than viewing things from a rigid (or dualistic, as cognitive psychologist William Perry, 1970, might call it) perspective, students have the opportunity to develop a kind of theoretical pluralism from which they can consider characters from more than one point of view. Here is an incident from one of Martha's classes that reveals the students' ability to view female characters from the feminist perspective.

We are discussing Virginia Woolf's *A Room of One's Own* during first period. Ever since we began discussing the feminist lens and *A Room of One's Own,* there's been a kind of edge in the air, especially with the male students, who are outnumbered by the female students by almost two to one. Adam and Tom look even more bored and contemptuous of the day's activities than usual. Kevin, an outspoken member of the alternative theater crowd, is sporting a new hair color (bright yellow) and seems particularly feisty.

"I'm, like, so over this Virginia Woolf," he says. "I think she goes way overboard; she overgeneralizes. She takes her argument too far, plus, she nit-picks."

Belinda asks, "What do you mean 'nit-pick' and 'overgeneralize'? How can she be doing those two things at the same time?"

Kevin looks a bit taken aback. "She just takes things a bit too far."

"Like what?" Belinda persists. "Can you think of anything from the text?" (This kid has been well-trained!)

"Like that part about Shakespeare," Kevin finally answers.

"What about it? Be specific." Belinda now seems to be doing a full-out imitation of her teacher.

"Well, you know. She says that Shakespeare writes for men and writes all these strong roles only for men. But in my opinion, when it comes right down to it, there are a lot of good women in Shakespeare. I mean, take Beatrice in *Much Ado About Nothing,* for example. I mean, need I say more? I mean, who could be a stronger role model than Beatrice? Didn't you just *admire* her? I mean, I did, and I'm a guy. Just think about Beatrice and you'll see. Virginia Woolf is whacked," Kevin concludes with a flourish.

"Yeah, Beatrice *is* something," Belinda concedes. "You've got a point there."

This classroom episode is illustrative of the lively and engaged discourse that was engendered by the introduction of the feminist lens. In addition to the students' evocation of the lens, this episode is also notable for the intertextual nature of the argument. That is, Kevin uses Shakespeare to support his point about Virginia Woolf. These students seem to be thoroughly in charge

of their own interpretations. They use the feminist lens to cajole each other into reconsidering a character from another perspective. How encouraging to think that they may be able to view their peers, teachers, and families from other perspectives as well.

CHANGING THE WAY WE VIEW TEXTS, "FEMINIST" AND OTHERWISE

Analyzing female characters is only one way the feminist lens can inform students' reading; the sociocultural context of texts also can be viewed through the feminist lens. This holistic view can illuminate classic texts, as it did in our reading of *Hamlet,* or more contemporary texts, as it did in our reading of *Native Son.* While the feminist lens can be fruitfully applied to any work of fiction, it may have different purposes when applied to texts authored by men and texts authored by women. As Elaine Showalter (1989) points out:

> Feminist criticism can be divided into two distinct varieties. The first type is concerned with woman as reader—with woman as the consumer of male-produced literature and with the way in which the hypothesis of a female reader changes our apprehension of a given text, awakening us to the significance of its sexual codes. Its subjects include the images and stereotypes of women in literature, the omissions and misconceptions about women in criticism, and the fissures in male-constructed literary history. . . . The second type of feminist criticism is concerned with woman as writer—with woman as the producer of textual meaning, with the history, themes, genres, and structures of literature by women. (p. 170)

While the feminist lens can be used profitably with a variety of texts, as I demonstrated with the rereading of *Hamlet, Native Son, The Great Gatsby,* and *Ordinary People,* among others, many feminist critics point to some seminal (one should excuse the expression) literary texts that serve as flashpoints for feminist scholarship and virtually demand a feminist reading. These texts include *The Awakening, A Room of One's Own,* "The Yellow Wallpaper," and "A Jury of Her Peers." (See Selected Literary Texts for a complete list of texts and authors.)

Whether to use these "feminist" texts or traditional texts in the teaching of the feminist lens is an interesting question for teachers. Texts that, for the purpose of this discussion, at least, I have labeled "feminist" help make the case to doubters or skeptics and broaden the discussion to larger considerations of women writers, women's ideology, and even whether there is such a thing as a "feminist text." On the other hand, the "eureka moments" of

Figure 5.1 From "Epithalamium—II"

unexpectedly altered vision through the power of critical lenses sometimes can occur more dramatically with texts that don't seem "loaded" or predisposed to a feminist treatment. In this case, as in many others, I promote the notion of "both . . . and" rather than "either . . . or" and try to include several different kinds of texts as I help students peer through the feminist lens.

Two classic texts that deal directly with feminist issues are "The Yellow Wallpaper" by Charlotte Perkins Gilman and *A Room of One's Own* by Virginia Woolf. I have used both to introduce the feminist lens to high school students and offer both strategies and examples of student responses in the next section. While the previous section focused on student responses to female characters, using the feminist lens, the next step is a consideration of an entire text from the feminist perspective.

I introduce the idea of a whole-text interpretation by presenting a concrete poem (see Figure 5.1). This gives students the opportunity to create a reading of an entire work but with a contained and literally concrete text. It gives them an opportunity to interpret a text as a cultural object. In addition, students are asked to consider a text about which they have not been able to form any investment, defensiveness, or prior expectations. The students, in small groups, note some of the physical features of the poem, for example, the serpent-like "S" that makes *he* into *she,* the "h" for *homo sapiens,* and the "e" for *Eve.*

They then try to regard the lens from a feminist perspective, in light of the basic tenets of the definition that they were given (see Appendix, Activity 11). In other words, they attend to features of gender, to what statements this poem might make about the relationship between the sexes, about the

prominence of the letter *S* and the cultural encodings about the relationship between men and women. Here are some samples of the students' readings of this concrete poem:

> She is better than he because the *S* creates a more developed, more aesthetically pleasing he.

> She makes he better.

> She is encompassing he.

> She is the center of the universe. He would be lost without she.

> She holds up he.

> Women are strong and bold but still bound by the central power of men. He is ever-present inside a woman controlling all of her actions and thoughts. He is the center of she.

> He is overshadowed by she.

> She is dividing his thoughts.

It's useful for students to see that they can disagree on the implications of a feminist reading of this poem—that is, for some it represents a feminist victory over male dominance; for others, it's just the opposite. Both interpretations rely on a feminist lens to provide meaning. Reading with theory doesn't necessarily lead one to particular conclusions about texts; it is not a prescription for dogma. Rather, it suggests frames in which a variety of interpretations can be articulated. There is no one single feminist reading of a particular text, and this exercise seems to illustrate that plurality of possibility fairly well.

After students discuss this initial foray into "reading feminist" with the concrete poem, we move to a consideration of "The Yellow Wallpaper," which, for a variety of reasons, is an important starting point for our exploration of the feminist lens. Annette Kolondy, for example, remarks on the significance of Charlotte Perkins Gilman's short story to feminist literary scholarship. First, "The Yellow Wallpaper" is an example of "previously lost or otherwise ignored works by women writers" (Kolondy, 1985, p. 144) that have returned to circulation as a result of feminist literary scholarship. Originally published in 1892, Perkins Gilman's short story was reprinted in 1973, and since then has become something of a feminist sensation, both widely anthologized and widely taught.

Kolondy remarks on the difficulty Perkins Gilman had initially publishing her piece as well as on the resistance it met with readers after it finally

saw print. As Kolondy points out, readers easily could have found similarities with Edgar Allan Poe's work. Yet, they did not display the same willingness to follow the interior tour of the disturbed mind of a trapped protagonist as they apparently had been with Poe's protagonists. Kolondy views "The Yellow Wallpaper" as a kind of meta-commentary on the sexual politics of literary reading and production. Kolondy points to the significance of the female protagonist whose imagination is limited by her proscribed activities and confinement and whose experience as described in the text cannot be read or interpreted accurately by her male audience.

"The Yellow Wallpaper," then, presents multilayered aspects of feminist meaning. It seems, therefore, to be a natural place for students to use the feminist lens. As a follow-up to the reading of the "She" poem (Epithalamium—II), I asked students to apply the feminist lens to write a brief analysis of the narrator, her situation, and perhaps Perkins Gilman's intent in writing the piece. In addition, they were to consider Perkins Gilman's audience and, finally, what meaning(s) they derived from the text.

Here are some of their resulting analyses:

> Perkins Gilman has written almost an essay on the position of women in the 1890s. The nameless woman in this story is forced to hide herself from her husband and the world. When finally able to let some of herself out, she is treated as though she is crazy and eventually she is. It is horrible to think that her true selves were so suppressed that opening up was so difficult that it drove her crazy.

> In the "The Yellow Wallpaper" the yellow wallpaper is a symbol for the control and dominance that man is exhibiting over women. The wallpaper is the distraction that keeps her from focusing on the things important to her. The distraction is control. In the end her tearing down of the wallpaper represents a step to break free, and that is what shocks her husband.

> In "The Yellow Wallpaper" Perkins Gilman is trying to show how trapped and controlled she feels in 1892. She is an intelligent woman who knows that men and women should be equal. She shows this in her story. John tries to control his wife in every way. He keeps her locked in a room and practically brainwashes her to the extent that she likes being locked up. In the end she seems to finally triumph when she locks herself in the room and starts creeping. She no longer follows his orders and crawls over him.

> It shows the effects of the repression of woman's will by what men saw as care and protection. John won't allow her to write or care for her

child, two important expressions of who she is, because he doesn't want her to get tired. She is the toy that can't be played with because it will decrease in value, that has no personal value because it can't be put to its use.

Charlotte Perkins Gilman, it seemed, was writing for her own struggle. The woman was trapped within the wallpaper while maybe Perkins Gilman was trapped in her words, thoughts, and positions. The woman was trapped, and the expression in her writing presents the struggles with her husband as a "Nora" (*The Doll's House*). They don't know her exact sickness or ailment but she is to stay in bed, cooped up to be better. But she needed to get out.

The fact that the woman appears to be content creeping around the perimeter of this dingy room is pathetic and for me is very far from triumphant, even if she did overcome some struggle. She is far from being at a point where she should be satisfied with her life. While Perkins Gilman does not say the reader should acknowledge the ending as pathetic, I don't think she should have to. The reader should be able to know that on his/her own.

This woman is treated like she was no more important than the wallpaper. Her husband has no regard for her well-being because, as she states early in the journals, she hated the wallpaper. By her husband forcing her into that room, telling her she be okay, he metaphorically pushed her into the wallpaper, a nonexistence. I believe Perkins Gilman wrote this story to help the women see their helplessness and inability to control their own destiny, although most probably, though, Perkins Gilman was crazy.

The narrator is unable to heal herself because she is controlled and acted upon by the men in her life. Perkins Gilman most definitely wanted to begin the world's consideration of the undermined position of females and begin to construct a new ideology regarding the gender roles in society. Perhaps she also wanted to restructure the internalized feelings of women in light of themselves.

I would like to look at this through a mixture of lenses. In order to do this story justice, I must mix historical and feminist lenses. The feminist lens may show an idea of oppression, but the addition of the historical lens shows triumphant behavior. Around the time when this was written and many years after, women were controlled by their "male figures." These figures could be fathers, brothers, husbands, or even sons. By showing how she is able to make a small step toward her

own decisions, this woman has made a statement to the community of women readers.

The narrator, nameless, a typical woman, had an undying devotion to her husband, the typical male in 1892. Struggling for the man in her life—living, breathing, surviving only for him—drove the nameless narrator to do the unthinkable. Perkins Gilman, being a woman writing this, then, had some intent: either to show the typical women or to snarl against it. Maybe to have *us* discuss it in class.

These are complex and perceptive responses to a fairly difficult text. Perhaps some of these themes of entrapment, manipulation, helplessness, and the veritable psychological war between the sexes (at least as represented by the narrator and her husband) might have emerged from students' readings if the feminist lens had not been a part of their interpretive repertoires. But the students' ability to view the text as a cultural artifact, as a challenge to a prevailing ideology, to amplify the struggles of the narrator to include all women, including Perkins Gilman's struggle as a writer, to understand the dialectical role the piece plays (e.g., "maybe to have *us* discuss it in class")—all these seem to demonstrate the influence the feminist lens had on their reading.

Now, I wondered, could they transfer these awarenesses from the classroom to the world outside of school? Could they apply this gendered way of reading into the ideologies that are inscribed in texts to the ideologies that are inscribed in our world? After all, isn't real-world relevance what reading with critical lenses is all about?

READING THE WORLD: FROM TEXT TO CONTEXT

There is a quiet revolt that seems to be gathering steam in Martha's fifth-hour literature class. They have just finished discussing Charlotte Perkins Gilman's "The Yellow Wallpaper" and are in the throes of their consideration of feminist literary theory. They are trying the feminist lens on literary characters they previously have met such as Curley's wife from *Of Mice and Men* and Daisy Buchanan from *The Great Gatsby*. They apply the feminist lens to *Hamlet's* Gertrude and Ophelia, and to a concrete poem (see Appendix, Activity 11).

Peter, seated near the front of the room, is absolutely bursting at the seams. For weeks he has fumed silently through the explanation of the feminist lens and through class activities that applied feminist theory to various literary texts, but now he seems unable to restrain himself.

"All this stuff is *construed*," Peter suddenly exclaims. "It's BS! Isn't there a *masculine* lens? This 'feminist lens' just isn't working for me."

"Of course it's not working for you!" Maria interjects from across the room. "You're a man. *You* can't see it, but *I* can see it because I live it." She continued firmly, "Besides, I was watching your face when we were reading about feminist literary theory. You were already shaking your head." (Peter shakes his head.)

"Yes, you were, Peter. You are so closed-minded."

A spirited discussion ensues between Peter and the other female students in the class who come quickly to provide unnecessary but welcomed support for Maria. The other male students listen in stony silence, refusing to rescue their self-appointed spokesperson, who is besieged by his frustrated female classmates. Peter doesn't seem to mind.

"I just don't buy it," Peter continues. "Just because a man writes a book doesn't mean he disses women."

"Oh, yeah?" says Robyn. "Let's take your favorite book—of course, by Hemingway. What about Lady Brett Ashley? How does Hemingway portray her?"

"Yes, as a sex object, of course," Peter concedes.

"See?" says Robyn triumphantly.

"Wait a minute," replies Peter. Now he's angry. "You mean, women *never* do that to men? Women authors *never* portray men as sex objects? You mean, there's no such thing as reverse sexism?"

"Peter," Maria is almost pleading. "Don't you realize you can only see things one way? It's because you're a man!"

"Well, you can only see things one way because you're a woman."

"No, that's not true. I have to see things from the masculine perspective because that is the perspective that dominates our society. And I also have to see things from a feminist perspective because I'm a woman." (I can't help but think of Du Bois's concept of double consciousness as Maria speaks.)

Peter shakes his head and tightens his jaw.

"Just try the lenses on, Peter! You can always take them off if they don't work for you!"

"I know, I know. But I still think it's construed."

This exchange, difficult though it was in many ways, indicates that, for these students, feminist theory has begun to move from the pages of their assigned reading to the edges of their world. This notion of reading the world and culture against the grain is, of course, one of the primary goals of introducing students to literary theory. While many students move from textual to personal on their own, others need encouragement and practice in reading culture against the grain, and resistantly, as feminist theory encourages us to do.

To help facilitate this movement from textual to personal, I created an activity to encourage students to read the world through feminist eyes (see Appendix, Activity 10). It begins by asking students to look at some cultural artifacts such as Mount Rushmore, the Miss America pageant, the coverage of the Olympic women's hockey team, the sexual scandal in the White House, the anchors of national network news shows, and Madonna's lingerie. They then are asked to "write a sentence about those objects or situations that contrasts a traditional perspective with the feminist lens." Here are some of the resulting responses:

Mount Rushmore

Reflects patriarchal society.

Shows the dominance of men in our society.

There are no females; are females just not good enough to be on national monuments?

Speaks to the fact that we had founding fathers and not founding mothers. And why? Because at the time, women weren't allowed to participate in society as leaders.

Let's face it! History glorifies men and excludes women. Period.

These are all Presidents; a woman should have been President by now.

Behind each of these men there is a woman who helped this country.

The Miss America Pageant

Women walk around parading on heels and dressed up like dolls for the benefit of the male public.

Puts physical attributes on a pedestal, but in a very unrealistic way; it's a breast issue!

Exploitation of women.

It's a display of boobs and pretty faces; women are trophies.

It is a tribute to our obsession with the physical appearance of women.

A blatant demoralizing objectification of women.

It's a parade of women who starve themselves so that a bunch of ignorant men can drool over them.

The Coverage of the Olympic Women's Hockey Team

What coverage? Are women's sports inferior?

The men's hockey team got way more coverage; it's just not fair.

A step in the right direction in equalizing women's attention in sports.

Only the men's was called the Dream Team. But the women's team was a Dream Team too.

We're getting there; at least there was a women's team. Now we can work on the coverage!

Women should have equal coverage!

There was virtually no coverage until it was clear that they had won.

In the end, it's a feminist victory that there even was a team.

The Sexual Scandal in the White House

The pillars of society are sexually corrupt.

More examples of how men dominate women.

Women are victims of the power relationships.

They treat Monica like she's an evil whore or something.

People are first to question the reliability of the women.

The Anchors of National Network News Shows

There are more men than women because the majority of Americans would listen to a man over a woman.

Men control the media.

Network news shows have attractive women in order to get people to watch.

People listen to a man's words but just concentrate on a woman's appearance.

More men are anchors because they are more able to travel without family constraints.

Only attractive females are allowed to play second fiddle to men.

Madonna's Lingerie

She sells herself through sex.

Madonna sells her body, not her music.

Two words—sex appeal.

Madonna is using her feminine characteristics to her advantage in gaining fame in a male-dominated industry.

GENDER TALES: READING THE TEXTS OF OUR LIVES

These responses are indicative of the students' ability to cast these cultural artifacts in the interpretive light of feminist literary theory. Yet the goal of teaching theory is not to produce discrete interpretations of individual artifacts; it is to help interpret, understand, and respond to our lived experiences. To encourage students to expand their interpretive skills from texts to object to actual events, the final section of this activity asks: "Can you think of anything that has happened to you or to a friend of yours in the past 2 weeks that could be better explained or understood through a feminist lens? Pick a partner and share stories."

Here are some of their resulting narratives:

Last night one young Sarah Church, my 10-year-old sister, watched the Miss U.S.A. pageant. I astutely informed her that such programming is a degradation, a blatant exploitation of America's desire to ogle at naked female flesh. She giggled and said it didn't matter because all the contestants are so stupid. One must question what kind of ideas this plants in the head of an impressionable 10-year-old: Stupid women are fun to watch. I shudder for the future.

I am a waitress and the other night I received a very large tip from two men. When I told one of my male co-workers about it, he made a very obscene remark along the lines of "What did I have to do for it?" It was a very dirty, nasty thing to say (I cannot repeat it in here), and even though it was a joke . . . it was not right. Feminist lens: He disrespected me.

Miss California didn't win the Miss U.S.A. pageant last night because she wasn't as pretty as Miss Massachusetts. Miss California gave a thorough, articulate answer to the question of what to put in a time capsule

and why. Miss Massachusetts gave an answer that was short and shallow.

I really can't think of anything at the moment . . . okay. At the charity talent show there were only two acts done by females. A feminist lens would say that our school doesn't encourage females to participate. Also no females received any awards for their efforts.

Yesterday in gym we were picking teams for handball. There are only two girls in the class and, like always, they were picked last. Everyone is okay with that because we all assume they are just bad at sports.

Recently, a very close friend of mine was in a shoe store browsing at shoes. She is young and rather attractive. She has a fresh look and a lot of charisma. She was approached by a middle-aged man who happened to be the regional manager of the store. Of course, he engaged her in small talk and eventually offered her a job. (At this point in the story, I think I knew why things happened like they did, but I guess I have a small optimistic hope for society. . . .) So she showed up for an interview, got the job, and went in for her first day. Looking nice, in the first 5 minutes of the job, she was told by an older woman coworker that the regional manager wants her to work at his store because her "looks" will attract business. Now this was not said in so many words, but my friend is very perceptive. Needless to say, that was her last day on the job, and my confidence in society was restored . . . partially.

Many females were angry at Channel 9's coverage of the high school hockey tournaments. The entire winners' bracket of the boys was televised, but only the championship game of the girls. Most people just think that the boys are more competitive, get more ratings, and are wanted to be seen more. But from a feminist point of view, they could say that Channel 9 has discriminated against women and was holding them down. They could say that this was an example of inequality and would place the blame on the boys in the tournament.

Being a cheerleader, I am subject to stereotypes every time I step into uniform. People joke about us; they automatically assume we spend more time doing our hair than practicing. They do not consider us athletes and believe the only reason we are cheering is to be close to the boys. Through the feminist lens, cheerleaders would be a part of a male-dominant society, only there to cheer the males to victory.

There was an interview with Madonna on the show "Ultrasound" on MTV. She talked about how people should listen more to her music

and concentrate less on her looks and actions. She hopes her new album "Ray of Light" will do this. She realizes that she is getting older and becoming less attractive so all that she has left is her music.

Last week I tried to help a girl carry a set of lights that were obviously too heavy for one person to try to carry. She did not want any help and almost dropped all the lights. I think she was trying to show me that my masculinity was not needed and she could do it herself. Through a feminist lens one would say that I was trying to keep women down by helping her and it was not my place to offer. I should have waited to be asked. A feminist would applaud the girl for trying to show that women can do jobs usually assigned to males. Even if the lights might have broken, it was OK. Women have to take risks in order to gain complete equality. The way I approached it was completely colored by gender. I was easily offended and very defensive. I feel I always have to be defensive nowadays. I am a Man.

When I was at work a couple of days ago, I was hosting at the front door. One of the waiters asked me to come into the kitchen to help him carry out some food to some of his tables. As I was walking out of the kitchen door, a different server offered to carry the tray for me, stating, "This is too heavy of a tray for a girl to carry." This made me very angry, and I felt hurt and discriminated against. I didn't say anything back to this server but was angered by the comment.

CONCLUSION

Feminist criticism is a political act whose aim is not simply to interpret the world but to change it, by changing the consciousness of those who read and their relation to what they read.
—Judith Fetterley, *The Resisting Reader*

Fetterley starkly reminds us that reading and teaching literature are political. Learning to read with feminist theory means learning to attend to the ideology of patriarchy, to the gendered nature of textual worlds, and to the significance of our responses as male and female readers. This chapter illustrates how feminist theory provides a critical lens that can transform students' visions as they interpret individual characters, as they evaluate the cultural significance of particular texts, and as they read and respond to the gendered patterns in the world. Finally, they also are able to see how their own gender affects their response to literary texts.

When the students were asked how their gender affected their reading, they offered the following comments (see Appendix, Activity 11):

My gender definitely did play a role in my reading of *A Room of One's Own*. It was difficult for me not to feel a bit defensive when it seemed that Virginia Woolf was attacking my fellow males and me. Still, after the initial impulse to defend myself and my gender, I was able to evaluate Woolf's ideas a bit more objectively. I believe that if I had been a woman, my reading would have been a bit different; I probably would have been a bit quicker to identify with Woolf. (Eric)

I find that my gender did not affect the way I read *A Room of One's Own*. Woolf presented an unbiased, fair argument and really presented nothing directly intended to bash males. The book mainly addressed problems and issues that cannot be denied; therefore, I don't believe one's gender can affect the reading of the text. Only when one addresses issues related to the text is gender an issue. Woolf presents a clear discussion of women's roles in fiction (writing) that gender cannot change. (John)

As a female, reading *A Room of One's Own* was a good experience for me. I thought the things she said about women and their roles in literature were very true and needed to be changed. I never felt that she was "bashing" men because that would not have been something I would have enjoyed reading. I am glad I read this book, even though it was boring (slow) in parts because the points made in it are all things women should be aware of. I think the book ends positively, for the most part, and does not blame men as the point of the book. As a female who does believe in equal rights, I think the book is appropriate and true. (Sara)

My gender did affect my reading of *A Room of One's Own*. When Woolf says a lot of comments that were made in the past, I felt really angered. When she describes how one man said that the dumbest man is better than the smartest woman, I was really offended. I don't believe it happens much anymore, but just the fact that it did angered me. If I was a man, I think I may have been angered, but not to the extent that I was because it is such a personal issue. My reading of the book was influenced by my gender because I took it very personally. (Jenny)

My being a female did affect how I read Virginia Woolf's *A Room of One's Own*. Although I personally don't feel as though I have been oppressed because I am a female, I understand that many other females

have. Therefore, I do think it is important that women should form a sort of silent sisterhood with each other. Because of this opinion, *A Room of One's Own* inspired me. It brought out many inner emotions such as anger, hurt, frustration. Through these emotions I came up with the thought that all women need to work together and rise above this oppression. By doing this, we do not need to pull men down, but we need to hold a firm grasp in order to pull ourselves up. Therefore, this novel was a great inspiration to me and taught me to care for all women. (Marissa)

I was not really affected by it despite my being male. The book itself seemed to be, for the most part, indifferent towards men; it dealt mostly with the women. (Justin)

I think my gender did affect my reaction because I could directly relate to some of the things she complained about. I have run into people with the opinions that women can't be as smart as men. I have never believed that, but I have felt the shock of people when I do well in math and science, traditionally male fields. Things are nowhere near as extreme for me as they were back in 1928, but that occasional feeling of being an oddity is much easier to relate to as a woman than I think it would be for a man. I think men are pretty aware of the big issues but sometimes I think they might miss the importance of little things such as books and tone of voice. As a woman I felt much more con-nected to what Virginia is talking about. (Shannon)

I think because I am female I understood her points better. I felt her anger when she wasn't allowed in the library. I know what she meant when she said women feel like they have to explain themselves through autobiographies. There were points in the book that her anger was more than what I have felt, and I thought, "Ouch, that's pretty harsh." If I were a man I would have probably taken offense to this instead of just letting it go. (Julie)

Yes, I think being a female somewhat influenced my reaction to *A Room of One's Own*. In many ways, I can see Woolf's arguments and problems because I can see them for myself in everyday situations. She talks about how men had all the freedom and women had none. Al-though this is, I believe, taken to an extreme, it is easy to understand these things because of my experience as a female. Also, I think it is easier to side with Virginia Woolf because I am a female and she is too. It's sort of like rooting for your own team because you are a part of it. (Jennifer)

I think my gender affected my reading of *A Room of One' Own* slightly. I noticed myself paying attention more to the successes (or at least what Virginia Woolf saw as a success) of women. I read those passages and felt proud of the individual women and of women in general. When Woolf talked about the injustices against women, it didn't affect me as much because I haven't experienced it. I sort of looked at those with a sense of "Look at what women have accomplished," but from a third-person sort of way. (Ginny)

I think my gender did play a part in my reading of *A Room of One's Own*. However, I think my personal experiences did even more so. I was able to focus more on the injustice of women being looked on as inferior. I think this is partly due to the fact that I have had or witnessed discrimination because I am female. I also think my "heroines journey" paper had a lot to do with what I got out of this book. Because I chose to write about feminist issues, I was able to relate to this book better. If I was a male I don't think I would have read the book the same way. (Stephanie)

Sure it did! People look at all things with their [own] view in mind; reading a book is no different. People may not always be aware of to what extent their point of view influences what they read, but with something as close to home as gender it is obvious. While some males were offended, or didn't like the book, females would be perhaps inspired. Different things speak to different people. (Johanna)

Yes, my gender influenced my reaction to *A Room of One's Own*. I found myself unable to connect with the characters and the story itself. However, I was able to understand the message but only by associating the novel with other notions of equality, such as racial equality. The reading was bland and uninteresting for me, and I drew little from it. (Dom)

I think subconsciously my gender affects everything I experience, including when I read *A Room of One's Own*. I felt bad for women in the past because of their hardships, but I also felt that Ms. Woolf needs to get over it. Times are changing and women are fighting for equality. I felt that because I live in such different times I didn't sympathize as much because I never felt like I've experienced [that] kind of oppression. I've personally never felt like I've been excluded from anything because I'm a woman. While reading this book, I had to constantly remind myself that women and Virginia were still being oppressed and they didn't have the rights I have today. (Erica)

Feminist literary theory provides a way for young men and young women to make meaning of their reading, their schooling, and their gendered place in the world. The process of recognizing textual politics and taking a stand with or against the authors and characters enables students to begin to articulate a more generalized sense of their places as women and men who create, out of necessity, feminist readings not only of texts but of worlds as well.

SUGGESTED ADDITIONAL READINGS

Buhle, M. J. (1998). *Feminism and its discontents: A century of struggle with psychoanalysis.* Cambridge, MA: Harvard University Press.
Buhle addresses the continuous conversation between feminism and psychoanalysis by looking at the commonalities and differences of both. She traces the evolution of two important theories of "human liberation" and describes how those theories inform each other.

Cronan Rose, E. (1993). American feminist criticism of contemporary women's fiction. *Signs, 18,* 346–375.
This article is valuable for its brief history of American feminist criticism of contemporary women writers and their works. The author analyzes many feminist works widely read in secondary schools in relation to the development and progress of American feminist criticism.

Eagleton, M. (1996). *Feminist literary theory.* Cambridge: Blackwell.
This is a classic work that gives the reader a thorough yet general view of feminist literary theory. The chapters are supported by good examples of popular literary works that are relevant to high school literary curricula.

Green, G., & Kahn, C. (1993). *Changing subjects: The making of feminist literary criticism.* New York: Routledge.
This book is an excellent collection of insightful autobiographical writings. The essays address how feminism has transformed the authors' scholarship, their lives, and their relationships with others. Of particular interest are the essays "Decades," "Reader, I Married Me," "The Long Goodbye," "Feminism, the Roaring Girls," and "Loss and Recovery."

Humm, M. (Ed.). (1992). *Feminisms: A reader.* London: Harvester/Wheatsheaf.
This book is a collection of writings from a variety of feminist writers and thinkers, who retrace the history of Western feminism from its beginnings in Britain and America to the 1990s. A chronology of feminist political events and the publishing of literary or theoretical texts introduces the reader to the work and its content.

Hunter College Women's Studies Collective. (1983). *Women's realities, women's choices.* New York: Oxford University Press.

This work is a complete and thorough introductory textbook that is an excellent first reading for a beginning feminist, and also could be used as a core text in an advanced high school English or humanities classroom. The chapters address both new scholarship on women and current controversial topics.

Pearce, L. (1997). *Feminism and the politics of reading.* London: Arnold Press.

Pearce looks at the complex and interdependent relationship between the reader and the text as she discusses and describes what it means to read a text as a "feminist." She extends her definition of text to literary texts, paintings, and art in general. She discusses the politics of gender reading and the emotional politics of gender reading.

Thompson, T. Studies in Shakespeare: Strategies for a feminist pedagogy. *Feminist Teacher, 8*(2), 67–74.

The author describes her rationale for teaching several works by Shakespeare from a feminist perspective. She describes her rationale for designing such a course, defines the course objectives, explains how to present her pedagogy to students, and takes the reader through a sample of a feminist analysis of *The Taming of the Shrew* as studied in her courses. Thompson includes a copy of her syllabus as well as a rich resource section.

Deconstruction: Postmodern Theory and the Postmodern High School Student

Between the unspeakable world and the text that will never shut up, where are we?

—Robert Scholes, *Textual Power*

Deconstruction is dumb. It's people who want to feel important trying to destroy meaning.

—Tim, Grade 12

No words could ever adequately express the emotion in the chamber of our hearts as we read. The novel deconstructs itself.

—Robyn, Grade 11, on reading *Snow Falling on Cedars*

THERE IS A MUSIC video that is relevant to the consideration of postmodern theory in the secondary classroom. The singer is Natalie Imbruglia, a relative newcomer to the music scene, and the video is for the song "Torn," which was on the top ten list for several weeks in 1999. In the MTV video, as in many music videos these days, the singer acts out a tortured and doomed relationship with a handsome male model pretending to be her boyfriend. They pace around a set designed to look like a twenty- or thirty-something's apartment right out of the TV sitcom *Friends* or *The Jerry Seinfeld Show*.

The premise for the video is a familiar one—two young people trying to figure out what happened to their once passionate relationship. Familiar, too, are the sunken eyes, flat bellies (heroin chic), khaki pants, and a melodic lament. But something is very different about this particular video.

As the singer proceeds with her song, construction workers arrive and begin to disassemble the set, taking it apart, *deconstructing* the "apartment" piece by piece, revealing it to be nothing more than a bare sound stage. The pretense of the assumptions on which the video was filmed, is revealed. Simi-

larly, the singer and the actor playing her boyfriend step out of their respective roles, revealing themselves to be two disconnected and unrelated people pretending to care about each other for the purposes of selling a CD. In a remarkably self-reflexive move, the video dissembles and the layers of pretense and the artifice of the music business are stripped away.

The willing suspension of disbelief that readers and viewers willingly engage in as we enter a constructed world of a text—whether a poem, a short story, a novel, a magazine article, a film, or a music video—is revealed, interrogated by the structure of the video itself. This re-examination of the constructs of the music video can serve as an interesting starting point for adolescents and deconstruction. After all, deconstruction invites us to "unravel" the constructs that surround us and to re-examine the relationships between appearance and reality.

DEFINING DECONSTRUCTION: AN EXERCISE IN FUTILITY?!

Even those literature teachers who may be well-versed in some of the other critical lenses we've discussed to this point may shudder at the notion of teaching deconstruction. Because it challenges the very iconic nature of the high school curriculum and the fixed meanings that have been assigned to canonical texts, it is a lens that most secondary language arts teachers have avoided. Additionally, as Lois Tyson (1999) points out, major proponents of deconstruction, such as Jacques Derrida, as well as their "translators" often attempt to explain the basic principles of the theory in language that is alienating and difficult. Finally, deconstruction frequently has been misunderstood as a destructive methodology, one that ruins our love and appreciation of literature with a superficial and trivial attack that amounts to nothing more than academic wordplay.

What *is* deconstruction and why does it inspire both fear and loathing? Here is one deconstructionist's hypothesis:

> Perhaps deconstruction has fired fear in people because it is difficult to define, and what cannot be defined cannot be pinned down and labeled; yet here lies the productive energy of deconstruction. In the very difficulty of naming and defining deconstruction, in the slipperiness of language that refuses to be pinned easily, deconstruction demonstrates and represents an understanding of language as vibrant and creative, opening up possibilities for meaning making. (Leggo, 1998, p. 186)

Despite his claim that it is difficult to define deconstruction, Leggo (1998) proceeds to offer a clear and lucid definition:

Deconstruction is a practice of reading that begins with the assumption that meaning is a textual construction. Perhaps even more useful than the noun "construction" is the verb "constructing" because deconstruction is a continuous process of interacting with texts. According to deconstruction, a text is not a window a reader can look through in order to see either the author's intention or an essential truth, nor is the text a mirror that turns back a vivid image of the reader's experiences, emotions, and insights. Instead, deconstruction is a practice of reading that aims to make meaning from a text by focusing on how the text works rhetorically, and how a text is connected to other texts as well as the historical, cultural, social, and political contexts in which texts are written, read, published, reviewed, rewarded, and distributed. (p. 187)

Deconstruction seeks to show that a literary work is usually self-contradictory. As Hillis Miller (1989) explains, "Deconstruction is not a dismantling of the structure of a text, but a demonstration that it has already dismantled itself. Its apparently solid ground is no rock but thin air" (p. 199).

In other words, a reader does not destroy or "dismantle" a text. S/he uses the interpretive strategies of deconstruction to reveal how a text unravels in self-contradiction. The source of those contradictions lies in the instability of language, the "undecidability" of meaning, and the ideologies that often are unconsciously revealed in the text. Appignanesi and Garratt (1999) emphasize this aspect of unintended meaning:

Deconstruction is a strategy for revealing the underlayers of meaning in a text that were suppressed or assumed in order for it to take its actual form. . . . Texts are never simply unitary but include resources that run counter to their assertions and/or their authors' intentions. (p. 80)

As Barnet (1996) puts it, deconstructionists "interrogate a text and they reveal what the authors were unaware of or thought they had kept safely out of sight." Barnet also offers a definition of deconstruction that is accessible to high school students:

[Deconstruction is] a critical approach that assumes that language is unstable and ambiguous and is therefore inherently contradictory. Because authors cannot control their language, texts reveal more than their authors are aware of. For instance, texts (like some institutions as the law, the churches, and the schools) are likely, when closely scrutinized, to reveal connections to society's economic system, even though the authors may have believed they were outside of the system. (p. 368)

Here is another good explanation of deconstruction, an explanation that also appears on the deconstruction handout (see Appendix, Activity 13) that forms the heart of the lesson described in this chapter:

> Deconstructionist critics probe beneath the finished surface of a story. Having been written by a human being with unresolved conflicts and contradictory emotions, a story may disguise rather than reveal the underlying anxieties or perplexities of the author. Below the surface, unresolved tensions or contradictions may account for the true dynamics of the story. The story may have one message for the ordinary unsophisticated reader and another for the reader who responds to its subtext, its subsurface ironies. Readers who deconstruct a text will be "resistant" readers. They will not be taken in by what a story says on the surface but will try to penetrate the disguises of the text. . . . They may engage in radical rereading of familiar classics. (Guth & Rico, 1996, p. 366)

"Radical rereading of familiar classics" and resistance to what a story says on the surface are consistent with the original aims of deconstruction. Yet, it is easy to jump to an oversimplified conclusion that deconstruction means nothing more than to "take apart" or "analyze." The term is now stripped of its once radical sheen. "Deconstruction" seems to be used and overused by pundits and commentators and CNN reporters, as in, "Let's deconstruct what happened in Kosovo," or, "Let's deconstruct this film." But these commentators don't unbuild or systematically examine the underlying constructs of, say, a political system or a leader or the ideology of a country or the motifs and conventions (binary or otherwise) that are presented in a film. They simply analyze their subject for its "deeper meaning," a move the deconstructionists abandoned. Deconstruction is a particular kind of unbuilding, one that takes into account the very nature, weight, and composition of the bricks or constructs it dismantles.

As Moore (1997) points out, many have confused deconstruction with destruction, a confusion that could be amplified by a careless use of the video that opens this chapter. Deconstruction is not a mindless dismantling; it is a mindful one. It is not destruction; it is de-*construction*. It is not, as Barbara Johnson (1981) has pointed out, "a kind of textual vandalism" (xiv). While deconstructionists discount particular sources of meaning, such as the binary oppositions of the structuralist or the notion that a text can have a single, fixed meaning, they do not assert that literature, or the study of literature for that matter, is meaningless. Rather, they posit that a text will yield multiple meanings, depending on the ways in which an individual reader may attempt to resolve the ambiguities and inconsistencies in the text.

Murfin (1989) points out that despite its difficulty, there is something almost irresistible about deconstruction:

Deconstruction has a reputation for being the most complex and forbidding of contemporary critical approaches to literature, but in fact almost all of us have, at one time, either deconstructed a text or badly wanted to deconstruct one. Sometimes, when we hear a lecturer effectively marshal evidence to show that a book means primarily one thing, we long to interrupt and ask what he or she would make of other, conveniently overlooked passages that seem to contradict the lecturer's thesis. Sometimes, after reading a provocative critical article that almost convinces us that a familiar work means the opposite of what we assumed it meant, we may wish to make an equally convincing case for our old way of reading the text. It isn't that we think that the poem or novel in question better supports our interpretation; it's that we think the text can be used to support both readings. And sometimes we simply want to make the point that texts can be used to support seemingly irreconcilable positions. (p. 199)

WHY ADOLESCENTS NEED DECONSTRUCTION

Despite the natural appeal of deconstruction that Murfin describes, the utility of deconstruction is fiercely debated even within literary circles. Even those who are firmly convinced of the usefulness of other kinds of literary theory readily dismiss deconstruction as both frivolous and difficult. Like a theoretical house of cards, deconstruction easily dismantles itself. It is often accompanied by or practiced with a cynical dismissive and even contemptuous tone. Barnet (1996) complains:

> The problem with deconstruction, however, is that too often it is reductive, telling the same story about every text—that here, yet again, and again, we see how a text is incoherent and heterogeneous. There is, too, an irritating arrogance in some deconstructive criticism: "The author could not see how his/her text is fundamentally unstable and self-contradictory, but *I* can and will issue my report." (p. 123, emphasis in original)

Others view deconstruction as passé, no longer a relevant or startling literary or theoretical enterprise the way it was when it crashed on the scene in the late 1960s and really took hold in the academy in the 1970s. In fact, in her *A Teacher's Introduction to Deconstruction,* Sharon Crowley (1989) quotes a newspaper clipping declaring that deconstruction is in fact "dead" (p. 24).

So, why should something so peripherally relevant even within the esoteric world of literary criticism be seen as something important for today's adolescents?

As argued in Chapter 1, contemporary adolescents are faced with a bewildering and confusing world, one that presents them with a dizzying array of social and psychological constructs, some as benign perhaps as the "Torn"

video, others more potentially destructive. Some have argued, in fact, that adolescence itself is a complicated and often cruel construct of our postindustrial
society. As Moore (1998) points out, in an argument for the relevance of
semiotics to adolescents:

> In adolescence students read the world that is represented to them, but they also
> socially construct a world in which they want to live, one that creates the identity
> they desire in the difficult landscape between childhood and adulthood. (p. 211)

Moore (1998) quotes McLaughin who emphasizes the necessity of theory in the classroom. It is "equipment for post-modern living" (p. 212), and
he contends that students are ready for it. They are adept at reading the
artifacts of their culture, a culture that "values image over reality, which has
replaced product with information" (p. 218).

Reading this postmodern culture requires that we reconsider which artifacts or elements of culture actually can and should be read. In other words,
we must refine "texts" to include a variety of forms, both print and nonprint,
literary and nonliterary. While the expansion of the concept of text clearly
can accompany any of the previous lenses we discussed and is indeed a requisite part of these critical encounters, it seems especially useful to redefine the
concept of text through the lens of deconstruction. The interrogation of the
meaning of text is a requisite part of deconstruction:

> [F]or many deconstructionists, the traditional conception of literature is merely
> an elitist "construct." All "texts" or "discourse" (novels, scientific papers, a Kew-
> pie doll on the mantle, watching TV, suing in court, walking the dog, and all
> other signs that human beings make) are of a piece; all are unstable systems of
> "signifying," all are fictions, all are "literature." (Barnet, 1996, p. 124)

In his invitation to English teachers to rethink the school subject of
"high school English," Bruce Pirie (1997) points out that English teachers
must learn to redefine texts and refocus the objects of study in our classrooms
to include the artifacts of popular culture and to learn to read them as texts.
As Garth Boomer (1988) argues, "If the profession of English studies and
English [instruction] is to survive and have any relevance for our students at
all, we need to expand our idea of texts to include the multivariate multime-
dia stimuli that surround them." Pirie quotes Boomer:

> Once "text" is conceived of as a cultural artifact, any text, past or present, classic
> or popular, fiction or non-fiction, written, oral or filmic, can be admitted to the
> English classroom for legitimate and regarding scrutiny, from the standpoint of

"Who made this? In what context? With what values? In whose interest? To what effect?" (Boomer, 1988, as quoted in Pirie, 1997, p. 17)

It is not only for the survival of our profession but for the survival of adolescents as well that our students, now perhaps more than ever before, need critical tools to read the increasingly bewildering and text-filled world that surrounds them. Those texts can range from the literary to a galaxy of artifacts in the external world. As the students in Martha's class recently pointed out, texts can include video, TV commercial, billboard, newspaper, magazine, expression of a face.

Additionally, adolescents are often, as psychologist William Perry points out, excessively dualistic in their thinking, which prevents them from being able to imagine, let alone sustain, multiplicity of thought. The dismantling of binaries, which is a requisite part of the deconstructive move, helps adolescents see the limits of binary thinking. As Terry Eagleton (1983) explains:

> Deconstruction, that is to say, has grasped the point that the binary oppositions with which classical structuralism tends to work represent a way of seeing typical of ideologies. Ideologies like to draw rigid boundaries between what is acceptable and what is not, between self and non-self, truth and falsity, sense and nonsense, reason and madness, central and marginal, surface and depth. Such metaphysical thinking, as I have said, cannot simply be eluded: we cannot catapult ourselves beyond this binary habit of thought into an ultra-metaphysical realm. But by a certain way of operating upon texts—whether "literary" or "philosophical"—we may begin to unravel these oppositions a little, demonstrate how one term of an anti-thesis secretly inheres within the other. Structuralism was generally satisfied if it could carve up a text into binary oppositions and expose the logic of their working. Deconstruction tries to show how such oppositions, in order to hold themselves in place, are sometimes betrayed into inverting or collapsing themselves or the need to banish to the text's margins certain niggling details which can be made to return and plague them. (p. 133)

The unraveling of the binary oppositions also helps unravel the ideology that set those polarities into motion and supported their production. As Derrida (1989) points out, it is through the dismantling of false binaries that we see the limitations of the ideology they were constructed to support. Deconstruction often is viewed as ultimately anti-authoritarian, a stance needed by those oppressed, as Barthes (1981) noted, by the overbearing and oppressive systems around them. Bonnycastle (1996) explains, "Deconstruction is often talked about as though it were primarily a critical method, but it is best understood as a way of resisting the authority of someone or something that has power over you" (p.112).

This anti-authoritarian aspect of deconstruction has natural appeal for

adolescents. But rather than simply stoking their rebellious fires, deconstruction provides adolescents with interpretive tools for critiquing the ideology that surrounds them. It teaches them to examine the very structure of the systems that oppress them and, in doing so, to intellectually dismantle them, thus making adolescents rebels *with* a cause.

The interpretive openness and flexibility of deconstruction are also appealing to adolescents. In the sense of multiplicity, the appeal is similar in some ways to deconstruction's sloppier cousin, reader response. As Leggo (1998) points out:

> What is especially commendable about deconstruction as an approach for responding to poetry is that readers, especially young readers in classrooms, do not have to be unnerved by self-deprecating fears that their responses to a poem are wrong. Instead of right and wrong answers, deconstruction encourages plural responses. Instead of a hidden meaning that must be revealed, the poetic text is a site where the reader's imagination, experience, understanding, and emotions come into play in unique performances. (pp. 187–188)

Finally, Tyson (1999) explains what deconstruction offers readers: "It can improve our ability to think critically and to see more readily the ways in which our experience is determined by ideologies of which we are unaware because they are built into our language" (p. 240).

DECONSTRUCTION IN THE LITERATURE
CLASSROOM: ONE APPROACH

Perhaps, as with this chapter, the most difficult part of teaching deconstruction to adolescents is the attempt to define it. Many of the definitions offered in the previous section seem understandable to adolescents. I incorporated the definitions into a handout (see Appendix, Activity 13). Many other teachers and I have found that when students are allowed to absorb and discuss the definitions and then paraphrase them, they are well on their way to a fairly solid understanding of this difficult concept. The lesson itself is designed as a kind of heuristic, first taking students through an explanation of deconstruction, then proceeding to deconstruct some common metaphors and the poem "Death Be Not Proud," a poem that is widely anthologized and that many students may have encountered already. Finally, working either alone or in small groups, they deconstruct a text of their own. This particular exercise focuses on the aspect of deconstruction that invites us to consider the fact that language is slippery and imperfect, or, as one teacher I know describes it, "Words wiggle."

To underscore the idea of words wiggling, we considered the following commonly used metaphors:

- Love is a rose.
- You are the sunshine of my life.
- The test was a bear.

If, as the deconstructionists argue, language reflects our own imperfection and the fact that words do wiggle, then metaphors may not have the effect the poet intended. Therefore, I asked students to "unpack" the metaphors and describe both the intended and unintended meaning. This exercise also serves as a warm-up for the next section, which asks students to deconstruct John Donne's "Death Be Not Proud."

The value of having students deconstruct a familiar and frequently taught poem is described succinctly by Guth and Rico (1996) in their introduction to a deconstructive reading of Wordsworth's "A Slumber Did My Spirit Seal":

> The following much anthologized poem is accompanied by a deconstructionist reading that clears away much of the apparent surface meaning of the poem. The critic then discovers a new and different dimension of meaning as the language used by the poet dances out its own significance. (p. 863)

As with the deconstructive reading of the Wordsworth classic, the intent of this part of the deconstruction exercise is to help students see how the commonly understood reading of a widely anthologized poem can unravel through the tools of deconstructive analysis. The analysis we used did not employ the deconstruction of the false binaries that Derrida originally offered. Rather, it focused on Barthes's notions of the "shifting meanings in the weave of the written text" (Moore, 1997, p. 77). Other critics have referred to the shifting and unstable nature of the meaning of a literature text as "undecidability." As Tyson (1999) explains, "To reveal a text's undecidability is to show that the 'meaning' of the text is really an indefinite, undecidable, plural, conflicting array of possible meanings, and that the text, therefore, has no meaning, in the traditional sense of the word, at all" (p. 252).

The handout asks students to contrast the author's intended meaning and the tools of traditional literary analysis with the consideration of how the poem might break down and work against the poet's intentions. They also are invited to consider places where the text falls apart, where the threads of meaning begin to unravel. The students attended to inherent contradictions in the poem and noted some of its internal inconsistencies. Here are some of their observations:

Why does he use the words "much pleasure"? He's trying too hard and we know it.

The poem breaks down when he offers that the only way to never have to face death is to die.

Do poppy and charms really make us sleep as well as death? Sorry. We're not convinced.

Death has power over us; it may be the only thing that does. He says "death shalt die"—but it never will die. He says "nor canst thou kill me;" but it can.

The poem is very contradictory. Donne attempts to dissect death and make it smaller, but the contradictions in the poem thwart the attempt and death ends up staying powerful and frightening.

First he asserts that a person can't die; then he describes how we do die.

He is trying to console himself, not the reader in this poem. I don't think he successfully manages to console either.

Though he says we wake eternally, he does not seem fully convinced that we do.

Although the poet is trying to convey that we must fight off death, that we are stronger than death, we, and he, cannot deny our fate.

The last line is completely indefensible. The punctuation also seems to add to confusion and may result in some unintended meaning.

The students then worked in pairs and reconsidered a reading on their own, using the heuristic of the exercise with "Death Be Not Proud." The texts they chose to deconstruct were wide-ranging and included some of those in Figure 6.1. For each text the students described their understanding of the author's purpose and then gave specific examples of how the text broke apart. Figure 6.2 is an example of how a student read against her own original reading to reveal possible conflicts in interpretation. Finally, students offered some reflective comments on deconstruction.

I like this lens although it is hard to determine what is and isn't meant all the time. The better authors seem to incorporate conflicting meanings to make the reader think.

Books	Poems
The Catcher in the Rye, J. D. Salinger	"The Universe," May Swenson
The Awakening, Kate Chopin	"The Executive's Death," Robert Bly
Heart of Darkness, Joseph Conrad	"My Papa's Waltz," Theodore Roethke
Native Son, Richard Wright	"Shall I Compare Thee to a Summer's
Of Mice and Men, John Steinbeck	Day," William Shakespeare
Romeo and Juliet, William	"Sonnet 18," William Shakespeare
Shakespeare	"Traveling Through the Dark," William
A Room of One's Own, Virginia Woolf	Stafford
Brave New World, George Orwell	"Kubla Khan," Samuel Taylor Coleridge
Sister Carrie, Theodore Dreiser	"I Saw a Chapel," William Blake
The Things They Carried, Tim	"I Wandered Lonely as a Cloud," William
O'Brien	Wordsworth
The Trial, Franz Kafka	"Ode to My Socks," Pablo Naruda
1984, George Orwell	"The Road Not Taken," Robert Frost
Snow Falling on Cedars, Dave	"The Unknown Citizen," W. H. Auden
Guterson	"Do Not Go Gentle into That Good Night,"
The Age of Innocence, Edith Wharton	Dylan Thomas
A Doll's House, Henrik Ibsen	"Bright Star, Would I Were Steadfast as
	Thou Art," John Keats

Figure 6.1 Texts for Use with the Deconstruction Exercise

Deconstruction is cynical.

Deconstruction is very hard to do. When I look at poems they do seem solid, with one main idea and no contradictions. It's extremely interesting, though. I'm going to keep trying, trying to see the contradictions.

Does deconstruction show flaws on the part of the writer or on the part of the reader?

I think that Tim O'Brien has written a story [*The Things They Carried*] that is at war with itself. In some passages he describes war's beauty and seems to love war, yet in other passages he claims to hate it. This is a war of themes. He hasn't decided for himself what he feels, so he puts his feeling on paper, using his emotions as truth and lying for evidence. He admits he can't decide how he feels many times, so I guess my main response is, If he can't decide, how can I, even? Who am I to say whether it is a love or war story?

Deconstruction reveals more than meets the eye. When viewed through the deconstructive literary technique, the main ideas, values, and beliefs of the author are revealed to be neither monstrous nor heroic. This view helps to understand hidden meaning not otherwise apparent.

Text: *The Awakening,* by Kate Chopin

When I deconstruct this text, here's what happens. I think the main idea the author/poet was trying to construct was:

This society's oppression of women is tragic, preventing their development and fulfillment in life.

But this construct really doesn't work. The idea falls apart. The language and construction of the text isn't able to convey what the author meant to convey. There are places in the text where it just doesn't work. For example:

In the opening island scene with the wives talking, Chopin wants to show how bored the women are (because they have nothing to do), but they end up seeming flighty and dull. Edna's suicide is supposed to be driven by society's oppression only, but her own weakness is very apparent as well.

So, in the end, even though the author meant the work to say

Edna was essentially the victim of an oppressive society.

it really said

Edna ended up killing herself; she had the option of living but just gave up.

(Optional) I'd also like to say that:

Kate Chopin probably had personal doubts that were involved in this book. Perhaps she saw herself in Edna and was attempting to justify her own failures through her.

Figure 6.2 Deconstruction Worksheet

On the whole, the lens of deconstruction works well with high school students. It seems especially compatible with their adolescent sensibilities, which are often characterized by a burgeoning iconoclasm. The students I worked with, for the most part, took readily to this lens. Yet there is a serious downside to using deconstruction. While all the other lenses we've discussed—reader response, feminism, Marxism—meet with their share of resistance from individual students for particular reasons, the resistance to deconstruction seems especially poignant and potentially harmful. In considering the use of deconstruction, teachers should consider the following incident, which occurred when I introduced deconstruction in Martha Cosgrove's class. After reading the incident, teachers may want to proceed with caution.

THE DANGER OF DECONSTRUCTION: RACHEL AND HER PLEA

The school year is drawing to a close and the students in Martha's senior English classes have been introduced to a whole variety of critical lenses. It's a dream class—lively, bright, engaged, and a bit feisty. They've taken the lenses seriously and have frequently challenged the usefulness and relevance of each theoretical perspective. But today will present a different kind of challenge. It is time to discuss deconstruction, one of the most difficult lenses of all.

The class thinks through the deconstruction handout. We read together the definitions of deconstruction. I try to keep the tone light—to keep us all from feeling overwhelmed. We're "playing with deconstruction," I say. We practice with metaphors (see Appendix, Activity 13) and discuss intended and unintended meanings. We then consider Donne's "Death Be Not Proud" and attempt to deconstruct it together. Last week, these students completed the AP test. This is probably important; we are not only deconstructing a traditional reading of the poem; we are in effect deconstructing the entire AP test and a particular way of interpreting literature.

The deconstruction exercise works well. Perhaps too well.

After we go through the entire lesson, including a deconstruction of a reading of their choice (see section, *Deconstruction in the Literature Classroom: One Approach*), the students seem both comfortable with their understanding of deconstruction and, at the same time, unsettled by that understanding. They get it, they can apply it—but they hate it. They seem uncomfortable. As if they managed to chew something unpleasant without choking but now the aftertaste is killing them.

Rachel is the first to speak. She has always struck me as a remarkably self-possessed young woman, confident and self-assured. Her high school education will be over in 2 weeks; in the fall she is off to the University of Michigan. Rachel is pragmatic. She takes a no-nonsense approach to many things, including literary interpretation. She seems mostly reality bound— firmly located in the here and now. She is also quite bright and has been able to engage enthusiastically in the varieties of literary discourse we've explored.

Rachel has never been shy about speaking her mind. She's one of the "beautiful people," the kind of girl other girls love to hate; she is part of the "in" crowd. She has gravitas, the weight of popularity surrounding her. She is from a fairly well-to-do family and seemed somewhat resistant to the Marxist lens when we studied it (see Chapter 4). She appears to be having a relatively successful adolescence and somehow doesn't seem particularly vulnerable to the vagaries of deconstruction.

Today, however, she is positively wailing. "Why did you teach us this?

I'm so sorry I know about this. How could you have told us about this? What are you trying to do—destroy us? How am I supposed to live with this knowledge? You've just demonstrated that everything we've learned up to this point has been a sham. Now what? Here I am at the end of my high school education, and now it seems as if everything I was trying to do is worth absolutely nothing. Nothing means anything. Is that what I'm supposed to believe? I feel as if all of my illusions have been torn down. And here we are left with nothing. What am I supposed to replace it with? It's not just what we've studied and how we've studied it—it's everything. Now I feel like everything I've done in school has been a big lie."

Martha and I are absolutely shocked and disturbed by this outburst. The class undertakes a metaphysical debate the likes of which I can't remember ever being a part of before. Sarah says that deconstruction should be taught at home. "We were going to find out all this stuff anyway, right? Better sooner than later."

The class erupts into a debate about whether deconstruction is indeed harmful to children. No one, oddly enough, is debating whether it is true or not—only whether children should learn about it. It strikes Martha and me as odd that the very students who generally make a very strong case for their full-fledged adulthood and the accompanying rights, are asking to have something be kept from them. It is not only during the class discussion that students' discomfort with deconstruction is evidenced. Although Rachel and Sarah bravely announced their issues with deconstruction in class, other students waited to confess their confusion in their journals. Kevin echoes Rachel's discontent in this entry from his reading journal:

Earlier this year, I wrote a paper on the literary lens of deconstruction and thought that I had a fairly complete understanding of the concept. I found out today that my understanding was not complete. I love it when I learn something new! I find literary deconstruction to be very thought-provoking but have unresolved conflict within me. I understand the concept of literary deconstruction, but isn't it destructive? The meaning of any work is questionable, but if some meaning isn't assumed, will we ever get anywhere? I have always believed that assumption is the worst thing any human can do, but educated assumption is necessary for humans to survive. We must assume that the sun will appear every morning and disappear every evening. We must also assume that we won't spontaneously combust. Assumption is necessary given human emotion. Assumption allows humans to feel comfort which helps them lead a contented life. If we didn't assume that the sun would rise in the morning, many would lead horrible lives. Many would constantly worry and suffer about the future. Yes, assumption is

not 100% safe, but nothing in this world is. One can safely assume many things if one takes the time to research things. Those who fear assumption are those who will end up on Prozac and Valium. Mental stability thrives in comfort. Uncertainty does not create comfort.

Are Rachel and Kevin right? Is deconstruction too potentially destructive for adolescents? The challenge doesn't arise as a result of the students' inability to understand such a difficult and complex concept. Oh, they get it all right. The challenge arises because understanding the implications of this particular lens is extremely frightening to them.

Perhaps for Rachel the fragile and artificial constructs on which she's based her entire high school career have come crashing down on her. Perhaps the lens of deconstruction has helped her see that her own adolescence and the constructs she uses to define it, may be as artificial and impermanent as the set of the "Torn" video.

Tyson (1999) addresses this byproduct, as it were, of deconstruction when she writes:

> As we have seen, deconstruction asserts that our experience of ourselves and our world is produced by the language we speak, and because all language is an unstable, ambiguous force-field of competing ideologies, we are, ourselves, unstable, ambiguous force-fields of competing ideologies. The self-image of a stable identity that many of us have is really just a comforting self-delusion, which we produce in collusion with our culture, for culture, too, wants to see itself as stable and coherent when in reality it is highly unstable and fragmented. We don't really have an identity because the word identity implies that we consist of one, singular self when in fact we are multiple and fragmented, consisting at any moment of conflicting beliefs, desires, fears, anxieties and intentions. (pp. 250–251)

CONCLUSION

> In my undergraduate English studies I was trained to look for meaning, like a beagle on the trail of a rabbit. The rabbit might twist and turn and hide, but if I persisted I could outwit the rabbit. Deconstruction reminds me that there is no plump rabbit seeking to avoid my capture and consumption.
> —Carl Leggo, *Open(ing) Texts*

The reaction of Rachel and her classmates to deconstruction serves as a caveat to teachers considering using this lens with high school students. While the privileging of "the personal" in reader response and the anti-ideology stances of feminism and Marxism seem to be developmentally appropriate

for adolescents, deconstruction is intellectually more challenging and psychologically more frightening for them.

In my experience, students have seemed uncomfortable with deconstruction. For the students described in this chapter, at least, deconstruction ultimately proved a somewhat dangerous tool for literary analysis, one that called into question the foundations of their personal identities and core beliefs. As Erikson, Marcia, Gilligan, and other theorists have noted, adolescents follow a developmental imperative to construct an identity. The fragility and instability of identity construction during adolescence apparently makes the nihilistic nature of deconstruction too painful for adolescents to integrate. Their ability to understand the theory was not in question. Rather, they just seemed too vulnerable to have their shaky foundations torn from under them. As Bonnycastle (1996) reminds us:

> If you go to deconstruction to find a set of values or a philosophy of life, you enter a world that is anachronistic and solipsistic—a world in which each person is essentially alone and cannot communicate with others, and social groups fall apart because they have no coherence. This, I think, is an almost impossible world to live in, but it is an interesting one to know about. (p. 115)

To be sure, high school students do, as Bonnycastle suggests, find the elements of deconstruction to be "interesting." And, despite its potentially nihilistic side effects, it seems to be worth teaching. Perhaps more than any other literary lens, deconstruction can inspire a particular kind of intellectual suppleness (M. Rose, personal communication, August 18, 1999). Like Marxism and feminism, it requires the reader to read ideology. Deconstruction helps students question the certainty of meaning without relying exclusively on the personal lens of reader response. Like reader response, it requires the reader to be an active meaning maker, but unlike reader response, with its sometimes sloppy overgeneralization and overapplication, deconstruction requires the rigor of a close reading.

Like the political prisms of Marxist and feminist literary theory, deconstruction teaches students to resist surface meaning and to read ideology— two critical skills students need to become autonomous and powerful adults. It is what they need to make meaning in the world and to evaluate cultural norms and expectations so that they do not merely succumb to them.

In *Textual Power*, Robert Scholes (1985) creates a metaphor for education. Students, he says, operate in an endless web of growth and change and interaction. As teachers, our task is "[t]o introduce students to the web, to make it real and visible for them" and "to encourage them to cast their own strands of thought and text into this network so that they will feel its power

and understand both how to use it and how to protect themselves from its abuses" (p. 21).

By introducing students to the power of deconstruction we may indeed put them at intellectual risk as they call everything into question. Yet with care and guidance, we ultimately may bestow upon them the "textual power" Scholes calls for by finally removing the artificial barrier between school knowledge and the knowledge that counts in the "real world." As Scholes (1985) states: "We must open the way between the literary and verbal text and the social text in which we live" (p. 24).

SUGGESTED ADDITIONAL READING

Derrida, J. (1991). *A Derrida reader: Between the blinds* (P. Kamuf, Ed.). New York: Columbia University Press.
    A useful and wide-ranging volume, it includes an extensive bibliography of Derrida's works and a short bibliography of secondary works.

Derrida, J. (1992). *Acts of literature.* (D. Attridge, Ed.). London: Routledge.
    This volume includes essays by Derrida regarding such figures as Joyce, Kafka, Mallarmé, Rousseau, and Shakespeare. A good reference to keep on hand and a comprehensive source of some of Derrida's most cited and discussed writings.

Foucault, M. (1984). *The Foucault reader* (P. Rabinow, Ed.). New York: Pantheon.
    This work includes an excellent selection from Foucault's extensive body of writings as well as some previously unpublished material.

Gutting, G. (Ed.). (1994). *The Cambridge companion to Foucault.* Cambridge: Cambridge University Press.
    Written for new readers of Foucault, this volume contains a systematic and comprehensive guide to his work. The selected essays in this collection discuss Foucault's critical influence on today's most recent and influential literary, historical, and philosophical debates.

Kennedy, A. (1990). *Reading resistance value: Deconstructive practice and the politics of literary critical encounters.* London: Macmillan.
    Kennedy provides deconstructionist readings of the works of such popular writers as Matthew Arnold, Robert Frost, Gabriel Garcia Marquez, George Orwell, Laurence Sterne, and William Wordsworth. In his readings Kennedy draws mainly on the works of Jacques Derrida and Paul de Man.

Sarup, M. (1989). *An introductory guide to post-structuralism and postmodernism.* Athens: University of Georgia Press.

Sarup provides an introduction to three very important figures in post-structuralism: Jacques Derrida, Michel Foucault, and Jacques Lacan. Sarup examines the effects of poststructuralist thought on the discourses of art, politics, psychoanalysis, and philosophy.

Tyson, L. (1991). Teaching deconstruction: Theory and practice in the undergraduate classroom. In J. M. Cahalan & D. B. Downing (Eds.), *Practicing theory in introductory college literature courses.* Urbana, IL: National Council of Teachers of English.

Written for teachers of literature, Tyson explains and demonstrates how deconstruction can be used alongside New Criticism to give students a very rich and complex view of literature and society. The author provides an explanation of how the principles of New Criticism already move inside deconstruction; she also contrasts and compares the two theories. Examples of deconstructing texts are included as well as exercises and assignments to be used in the classroom to prepare students to deconstruct a text and to actually go through the process of deconstructing.

Williams, J. (1986). The death of deconstruction, the end of theory, and other ominous rumors. *Narrative, 4*(1).

In this article Williams responds to the recent debate in literary circles regarding the death of deconstruction, yet notes the subtle institutional acceptance of this theoretical view. Williams sketches out a brief history of the course of deconstruction and the significant role that it has played in the field of literary theory.

CHAPTER SEVEN

From Study Guides to Poststructuralism: Teacher Transformations

> We may claim to scorn theory, but the moment we begin teaching, we enact our understanding—our theories—of what language and communication are all about and what kinds of reading, writing, and talking deserve student effort. Theory is there, although it may be either explicit or submerged, sensible or chaotic.
>
> —Bruce Pirie, *Reshaping High School English*

> Our practices exist by virtue of our theories.
>
> —John Willinsky, *Teaching Literature Is Teaching in Theory*

AS WE HAVE SEEN, teaching literary theory to high school students can have transformative power for the students, but what does it do for their teachers? The focus of this chapter is Martha Cosgrove, an English teacher whose classroom is featured throughout the other chapters of this book. Martha's story provides evidence of how literary theory can transform a teaching life. For while Martha's journey is extraordinary in many respects, she is—in training, background, and disposition—like thousands of other secondary teachers across the country. In Martha's story, then, lie the patterns and possibilities of professional and personal growth that are relevant for all current and future teachers of literature.

MARTHA'S STORY

Martha currently teaches both "regular" and advanced placement English courses at a large, comprehensive high school in a white-collar suburb where both students and teachers are mostly White, mostly Protestant, and mostly middle to upper middle class. Over 25 years ago, Martha and I began our

high school teaching careers together. We graduated from the same teacher preparation program at a large midwestern university and were hired at the same suburban high school.

Even in the early days of her teaching, Martha was as orderly and controlled as her carefully created teacherly appearance—long blonde hair constrained in a tight bun, tailored and monochromatic clothes. Although probably neither of us knew it at the time, her focused teaching, disciplined classroom environment, and approach to literature probably would fall into what we would now call a New Critical stance, while I labored in a classroom a floor below her following a messier, noisier, more "student-centered" approach. (I should point out, however, that the differences in our teaching styles was probably attributable to personality and instinct rather than to an explicit and acknowledged theoretical position, since critical theory was not a part of our teacher training program either in our English courses or in our methods classes.)

Although, by all accounts, she was an effective and dedicated teacher, Martha would be the first to admit that there was nothing particularly innovative or constructivist about her classroom in those early days. She taught American literature by relying heavily on her tenth-grade anthology as well as on her knowledge and experience with canonical texts. She taught literary terms, interpreted texts for symbol and themes, assigned study guides for novels, tested for vocabulary, and was especially adept at teaching her students to write academic papers. Martha was a fairly strict teacher. Her manner was didactic; her approach to literature was text-centered. There was little room for personal response in Martha's classroom. Martha concurs with this description of her early days of teaching. Recently when asked, "How do you think you might have described your role as a teacher 20 years ago?" she replied:

> I suppose the natural reply is that I expected to teach content to students, to pour information into their heads. Or, perhaps, that I didn't think much about it. I think I would have said I was teaching kids books. And, particularly, I was teaching American books that both informed and influenced who we (I was part of that equation too) were and would become as part of a uniquely American culture.

The first major challenge to Martha's pedagogical paradigm was her foray into interdisciplinary teaching. Teaming up with an American history teacher in the late 1970s, Martha attempted to create a thematic, interdisciplinary approach to the teaching of American literature and American history. She began to explore beyond the boundaries of her content area and became interested in art, art history, American history, and music. This inter-

disciplinary orientation significantly expanded Martha's intellectual horizons as well as her approach to teaching literature. She developed a more inquiry-based approach to literature, inviting students to develop their own questions about texts rather than memorize answers to her questions. She also abandoned her strictly chronological approach to literature in favor of a thematic approach that focused on the relationship between historical events and the literature of the time.

In the early 1980s, Martha left teaching for a few years to raise a family. When she returned, it was not to the conventional high school setting she had left but to an alternative literacy center to work with nontraditional students. Martha taught adults to read and worked with students who had dropped out or had been forced out of high school. As Martha worked with these students, she quickly realized that the teaching strategies she had perfected for her sophomore English class had little value in this setting. Her allegiance to the "subject" of English shifted as she focused more directly on the literacy skills her students needed to improve their lives.

After a couple of years at the literacy center, Martha taught remedial reading at a junior high school in Minneapolis. Challenged by the diversity of her students as well as the low level of their skills, Martha says it was at the literacy center that she learned "to take the temperature of a group and adjust immediately. It was do that or die a thousand deaths!" Again, Martha was forced to rely on her reading of her students' needs rather than on her disciplinary knowledge. She continued to radically revise what it meant to be an English teacher.

Martha eventually received an offer to return to teach high school. When she did return to the very same classroom where 20 years earlier she had begun her teaching career, nearly everything about her teaching had changed. Martha had a different sense of purpose. She was no longer a broker of cultural goods, a steward of the literary heritage of the United States. She had become a catalyst for literacy, a facilitator of change to learners who might be wildly divergent in their skills, aptitudes, experiences, and motivations. She also began to alter her notion of the students' role in the classroom. For Martha, her students were no longer dutiful note takers of lectures; they were astute consumers of literature, acutely aware of their own educational needs and interests.

Martha was always a sensitive and voracious reader, and her tastes gradually had become more eclectic as she pored over book reviews and haunted local bookstores. She ordered classroom sets of novels by Toni Morrison, Barbara Kingsolver, Anne Tyler, and Virginia Woolf to add to her collection of Steinbeck, Hemingway, Faulkner, and Shakespeare. She had continued to develop her interest in thematic approaches to teaching literature as well as her interest in multicultural literature. While much about her teaching had

already changed, Martha was ready to reshape her curriculum and to explore new areas of inquiry for herself and her students. Martha's desire to restructure her year-long Modern Novels and advanced placement classes inspired her to consider multiple-theory approaches to teaching literature. When I asked her if she was interested in incorporating literary theory into her curriculum, she agreed enthusiastically.

The results of our collaboration form the core of this text. Many of the lessons we created and taught together are described in other chapters of this book. The voices of Martha's students can be heard throughout all of these pages—through classroom vignettes as well as through the students' writing. This chapter focuses on Martha's professional and personal transformations, which Martha and I both firmly believe were a result of teaching literary theory. Many of those changes will be described in her own words.

CLASSROOM TRANSFORMATIONS

When Martha began teaching, her classroom was arranged in the traditional configuration of desks in straight rows with a big teacher's desk, as Nancy Atwell (1998) describes it, up front. There were a few standard issue classroom posters from the Perfection Form company hung symmetrically along the wall. The only personal touch was the vase of flowers on the teacher's desk, kept in fresh supply by Martha herself. Now, over 20 years later, the only sign of physical continuity in Martha's classroom is that vase of flowers, still filled weekly with daisies or daffodils. Even in her description of the physical appearance of her classroom, one can detect the dramatic nature of Martha's pedagogical transformation.

> My classroom. I hope it is lively and infused with the essence of students. Lively, because there are kites hanging on the ceiling, posters on the wall, the stuff teachers do to try to pretend they're not teaching in a shoe box with the lid on. But the "essence of students" is the most interesting part. Kids "have to" send postcards if they go on vacation and miss class; and kids "have to" send me a postcard once they settle in college—which actually tells me a lot about whether I'm hitting the mark with their transition from high school to college—so there are a jillion postcards on the wall and cabinet doors. The bottoms are all curled up because current students are always interested in reading my mail. Who sent which postcard, etc. Several years, students have chipped in money and bought me a kite as a gift—which makes for a pretty swell collection. Last year, I figured out if the kids signed the tail it would be a cool, permanent remembrance—and I had them include

a favorite passage of poetry. Very lovely. Then there are the senior pictures that are on the side of the file cabinet. With the poster of *Hamlet*. The kids have slowly invaded. I try to keep Yorick's skull still visible, but we're heading on the second layer so I don't know how long that will last. Chairs are in a u-shape so kids can see each other as they discuss. I most often pull a seat into the circle and am part of the discussion, not the stand-up-tall teacher person. But I've found that this changes from year to year, given who the kids are and where they are in their ability and need to have a teacher as an authority. Regardless of where they start in the need for a *teacher* teacher, I'm moving off to the side.

I'd say the movement of the teacher is a very interesting proposition. I remember the year we moved me out of the center of the classroom. My reaction was interesting—because I felt very marginalized, but also because I thought that was a very good place for my students to have me be. Lots of cognitive dissonance on that one. So now I have to get a read on where kids are physically and place myself there in the room: at the overhead, on the table, on the orange chair on the side, at a student desk pulled up in the front of the room, at a student desk among students, participating, at a student desk among students, mostly observing—locations that seem to rank the impact of my presence from most to least. And my place comes and goes, given difficulty of material and interest of students in selections as well. All very complicated, this teaching business.

THE CHANGING ROLE OF THE TEACHER

Martha's focus on her students is clear from the above description, as is the change in her perception of her role from center stage to "off to the side," as she says. Here is how she describes her current role with her students:

It is hard to think objectively about my role as a teacher today. I feel more like a "nudger" of minds. Or is that too gentle? I am most aware of sensing how far or how hard I can push them—when to fall back, when to encourage, when to/how to tell them they're not doing very well. This varies, both with the individual and the group.

I hope students see me as a collaborator and a co-conspirator in their learning. When I've taught kids as juniors too, this is easier because we have a relationship to draw on. We also have successfully navigated a difficult piece of learning and writing in junior year, so we've weathered some storms together and prevailed.

I do work pretty hard in placing expectations outside my personal preference; that has a big impact on the relationships piece. I want kids to understand I am on their side but try to avoid an adversarial model. If there is a battle I want to be on the kid's side. Against what? A piece of literature that is difficult to understand; that would be okay with me. Or against the *College Board;* that is very okay with me. But it is not the kid against me.

CHANGING ONE'S TEACHING GOALS

Through the description of Martha's classroom as well as her explanation of her role as a teacher, it is clear that this "nudger" has significantly shifted her stance from a text-centered teacher armed with vocabulary texts and study guides to a facilitator of learning who keeps the students, not the text, squarely in the center of attention. Of course, some aspects of Martha's teaching remain unaltered: her emphasis on teaching writing, on preparing students for college, on the respect and enthusiasm she wants to convey for literary texts. But much about her teaching *has* changed, including, not insignificantly, her ability to describe her goals. For teachers as well as for students, theory makes the invisible visible, the unsaid said. So, the *theoried* Martha describes her current goals for teaching this way:

> My goals for kids, then, are to help them develop the writing skills necessary to navigate their writing needs immediately in their freshman year at college—to have them understand they are unfinished as writers and learners, so they're not surprised to learn they don't know it all(!). And to help them become independent thinkers, to know that they have a "way in," a strategy (several actually) to use to work on a text—literary or otherwise. I want them to be open, to acquire patience. So they might understand that if they can reserve judgment there may be some important rewards in reading and learning. I want them to understand that to like something and for it to be good are not the same thing. But they can be. I want students to understand that good learning is not necessarily painful.
>
> So these goals have changed in that I didn't consciously understand much of this 20 years ago. I'm a pretty instinctive teacher. Actually, being aware of this stuff sort of spoils it for me. But never mind. So goals 20 years ago were much more text-centered. Now, I want kids to understand what happened in a short story, why it happened (motivation of characters stuff), the theme, how the story reflected what was happening in a larger intellectual context in this country (the Ameri-

can studies stuff), how different art forms reflected the same instincts and historical events. It's not that I don't want kids to do this kind of traditional study. I want them to do more, and the balance of power has shifted.

THE ROLE OF LITERARY THEORY IN MARTHA'S TEACHING GOALS

How much of this shift in "the balance of power," as Martha describes it, could be ascribed to the teaching of literary theory? And, more generally, how can literary theory inform the pedagogical goals of other teachers? For Martha, teaching literary theory has clearly transformed her teaching goals.

> For me, teaching literary theory is about teaching kids metacognition and encouraging flexibility in thinking. It's about giving them power as learners, because literary theory enables them to know what they are doing while they are doing it. It's a bit like the Oz metaphor—lifting back the curtain and seeing the Wizard of Oz at work. And I feel very much like the wizard who exclaims, "Ignore that man behind the curtain!" One of the magical parts of teaching for me is creating circumstances for students which result in a magical act of understanding, of realization. When you give them the keys to even some of that magic, it is not magic anymore. (Unfortunately, this actually becomes a pretty big downside.)

As Martha indicates, teaching literary theory dislocates the teacher in meaningful ways, requiring her to reconsider where the source of the "magic" comes from. It places the source of that magic on the theoretical and interpretive abilities of the student, rather than the teacher, to construct meaning. Twenty years ago, Martha expected to be the sole magician, "the Wizard," as she put it. Now she focuses on "creating circumstances for students which result in a magical act of understanding, of realization." As a result of her multiple-theory approach, Martha's teaching has clearly become more student-centered, more constructivist. Her focus is not on refining the magic of her own teaching performances, but on the magic of watching students who are in control of their own meaning making.

Both Martha and I are confident that this constructive shift will occur in the classrooms of all teachers who adopt this approach. This shift in pedagogy is perhaps the inevitable result of teaching with theory. As Slevin and Young write in their introduction to a collection of essays called *Critical Theory and the Teaching of Literature: Politics, Curriculum, Pedagogy* (1995):

> This [book] asks us to see our students not as the receivers of our theoretical knowledge, but as participants in our making of it. . . . Teaching literature and getting students talking/writing are inseparable in this view of things; students play a central role as the makers of the meaning of literary education. (p. x)

RETHINKING THE CURRICULUM

Martha also has changed the structure and the content of her literature classes. No longer feeling obligated to deliver an expected standard fare of canonical pieces, Martha includes in her courses a wide range of literature, from the poetry of John Donne to Adrienne Rich, from *Heart of Darkness* to *The Things They Carried.* She ruefully meditated on how her use of a literary anthology has changed since she began teaching AP English:

> Having just sent out the "Welcome to the 10th AP Class Summer Reading Meeting" invitation, I realized, of course, that this has been in the making for a decade. Seems to be an institution. But today, in collecting the "big purple" (their literature anthology), kids don't even remember what they read from it. Frankly it's been nothing more than a dust collector in their lockers or a doorstop in their bedroom, if they ever brought it home. Actually, the only thing they read from the anthology now is an excerpt from *Beowulf.*
>
> Remember 10 years ago when we knew we *shouldn't* be using an anthology but it seemed that too much was at stake if we wanted kids to perform well on an AP exam at the end of the year? So, it takes a *decade* and a whole new way of teaching to make an anthology *really,* fundamentally, truly irrelevant!
>
> What this means for change in education is terrifying! Molasses is speedy in comparison.

Martha's course is no longer arranged chronologically but through a series of inventive multigenre units such as "The Mind and Its Metaphors," "Protecting Place," "Questions and Resistance," and "Lies in Quest of the Truth." If there is any other organizing frame, it is the concept of multiple perspectives and the use of theory to achieve that multiplicity.

Martha now requires her students to engage in different ways with the literature she teaches. Gone are the mandatory study guides and pop vocabulary quizzes. Students maintain reading journals and write a variety of response papers as well as critical essays. Martha frequently asks students to "put on their critical lenses" through assignments that range from theory

relays (see Chapter 3 and Appendix, Activities 6 and 14, for example) to analyses of cultural artifacts. She invites them to pursue independent research and reading. Students convene symposia on critical theory and lead class discussions. They meet after school to weigh the usefulness of particular literary theories to individual texts and to plan strategies for their class presentations. In sum, the nature of academic work in Martha's classroom has changed completely from her early days as an American literature teacher. These assignments echo many of the changes in student work that Beverly Sauer (1995) called for when, in summarizing the results of a 1992 Institute on Teaching Theory by NCTE, she asked: "How can student assignments reflect the kind of theorizing we would like students to do?" (p. 347). Sauer concluded that the kinds of assignments that would encourage theorizing included "foregrounding issues of power, refiguring traditional courses, enabling students to engage in critical debate with their peers, and understanding the role of texts as cultural artifacts" (pp. 348–349).

Although Sauer and the other participants of the Institute on Teaching Theory had college students in mind when they explored these questions, Martha's high school students ably engaged in the kind of theorizing that Sauer and others envisioned. So, for Martha and her students, studying literature now means theorizing about it. They have the opportunity to achieve "textual power" (Scholes, 1985).

MARTHA ON THEORY AND HER STUDENTS

But is textual power necessary and obtainable for all high school students? While the premise of this book is that the answer is a resounding yes, Martha frequently asks herself whether theory is both useful and appropriate for the broad range of students that inhabit her classroom. It is a fair question, one that many teachers inevitably will ask. Central to the viability of critical theory to high school students is the assertion that it can and should be taught to students with a wide range of abilities. Theory can be especially powerful for those students who feel the most powerless, students whose performance in school, family background, or other factors put them on the margins of the academic and social life of the school. In fact, it is for these very students that theory may be most important. Literary theory may help students to "read" the factors that contribute to their status in school, may help them reflect on their own investment in learning, and may give them additional interpretive authority.

There are many factors that may determine a student's receptivity to reading with theory. Over the past few school years, Martha has learned that

some students enthusiastically embrace critical lenses while others completely reject them. Some students may respond well to particular lenses yet be resistant to others. Here is how Martha assesses different students' predispositions to theory:

> Kids who are systematic like this stuff. It's a way of controlling what usually is a subjective discipline for the "right-brained," mathematically inclined, computer science kids. I don't believe you have to be a really "smart" kid to do this, but it might be about how much attention kids are willing to devote to a single work.
>
> Kids are resistant to theories that are incompatible with their own opinions. I hesitate to say "philosophy" or "world view," because I don't think in most cases it is that well thought out. I'm thinking about the resistance to feminist theory. The students aren't as panicky about Marxism, even though they are certainly all good capitalists, so maybe my explanation about incompatibility isn't entirely correct. We do talk about that fact that they don't have to *adopt* the philosophy behind the lens to use and understand it. But nevertheless, feminism is a very potent issue for 17-year-old kids. The resistance has more to do with the great right-wing conspiracy to demonize the feminist movement, I think, and I am only partly kidding.
>
> So, kids are resistant to particular lenses for particular reasons. But are some resistant to lenses altogether? Probably the kids who don't want to analyze poetry to death. It's about breaking with the magic. And, as I've said before, I have very serious reservations about doing this. Those reservations seem more serious the more I think about them.

CRITICAL THEORY BEYOND THE CLASSROOM

One of the primary claims of this book is that critical theory can travel with adolescents from the literature classroom into the rest of their lives—whether it's to inform their viewing of an MTV video or to reframe their thinking about stereotypes. As teachers, we want our students to critically read the world; we want them to be able to make personal decisions (or at least adopt a stance) that reflect a keen understanding of their location (and degree of complicity) within a variety of competing ideologies and possibilities.

If learning theory can change adolescents' perceptions and inclinations, could it do the same for their teacher? As we have seen, Martha has changed considerably since she began teaching, but can any of those changes be attributable to reading literary theory and then infusing it into her high school

literature classroom? I wondered whether Martha saw the influence of theory in other aspects of her life.

> Critical lenses and my life. It definitely is part of my thinking as I am selecting materials in my other courses. The slippage of literary theory into my humanities course is *very* interesting to me, both in selecting materials and in watching how kids talk and think about viewing a text from a particular perspective that they don't realize is actually a defined literary theory. In a second or third year that I teach that course, lenses will have a place. Do I think about how lenses color my view of the 1999 Clinton impeachment vote, for example? Yes. Do I think about how lenses color the way John [Martha's husband] sees the world and isn't aware of it? Yes. It's automatic.

This year Martha experienced several profound changes in her personal life. She and her husband had bought her childhood home from her widowed mother. They had raised two children in that home; her 17-year-old daughter sleeps in the same bedroom that Martha did as a girl. Never a risk taker, Martha preferred what she called "the safe route." As she put it, "I haven't had to learn the name of a new street for the last 30 years." Bound in her childhood neighborhood, Martha seemed, if not content, at least complacent in her surroundings.

Lately, however, Martha reported a growing restlessness. This spring Martha and her husband bought a home in another part of the midwestern city where they've both lived all their lives, moving her family out of the neighborhood she's known since childhood. At the same time, Martha applied for teaching positions outside the school district where she had been teaching off and on for the past 25 years.

Is Martha experiencing a mid-life crisis? Not exactly—at least she doesn't think so:

> Why all these changes this year? Good question [laughs]. Well, I'm sure they have been building up for a while. Teaching this stuff to kids made me realize I needed to put my money where my mouth was. Not that I was very conscious about all this stuff. But here I was asking kids not to remain stuck in their physical and conceptual worlds and yet I was stuck in mine. I live more easily with ambiguity now and, as our friend Emily [Dickinson] once said, "I dwell in possibility."
>
> Moving, of course, has been the most dramatic manifestation of all this theory stuff. Not only did I feel more courageous about the idea of it (and I'm still thinking about what all of that means), but I had to confront my old teaching life in a concrete way. Looking at

boxes in the storage closet—those boxes filled with folders of vocabulary and study guides and even a Gershwin tape—and knowing that even if I ever taught American lit again. . . . But what would be the point? I took those boxes to the trash without even opening them up.

Of course, it would be absurd to conclude that teaching critical theory was the direct cause of all the significant changes in Martha's life or to claim, like a traveling snake oil salesman, that teaching theory will not only "make your students learn better but can make your life more interesting, too." But, as Martha repeatedly points out, the flexibility of thought that multiple perspectives demand cannot be limited solely to the reading of texts; it transfers to the reading of worlds as well. Once one is able to sustain the possibility of several different meanings of a novel, short story, or poem, other possibilities—not just ways of reading but ways of living—seem to emerge.

COLLABORATION

Although Martha and I had known each other as colleagues and as friends for many years, this new partnership, which seemed to yield such interesting lessons for students, enriched our own teaching as well as our relationship, both in and out of the classroom. Like Theodore Sizer's (1986) Horace, Martha teaches largely in isolation. Good teaching ideas occasionally float like rumors into the teachers' lounge. Martha wants to pursue these teaching ideas but finds she has no time during the school day to observe other teachers, let alone to share ideas or plan lessons. Attending professional conferences doesn't seem to provide Martha with the camaraderie or intellectual partnership she craves. In some ways, integrating literary theory into Martha's literature illustrated for us not only an innovative approach to teaching literature but a model for working together to create curriculum. In a recent conversation with Martha, she reflected on our collaboration:

> I think the way my teaching has changed, really, is that our collaboration has encouraged me to place the student in the center of the classroom. No, it's really forced me do to that, and I think that is a good thing. For you, it has always been the student first, and all else follows. So, anyway, 5 years later students keep creeping to the forefront. Now they've arrived. That is quite an achievement, actually.
>
> It is fabulous to have another person as desperately interested in what's happening in my classroom as I am. All the talk about the isolation of teaching, the lack of time to reflect, all of Horace's compromises. Lots of that is dramatically diminished by our collaboration.

You also allow me to feel less apologetic about what I do, about how much time I spend doing it. You give me permission to do many things I've wanted to do but was not courageous enough to do on my own. To have kids like what and where they're learning. To allow kids to do difficult things. To create lessons I'm not sure will work out. To think about how many times we've started literary theory and not been satisfied. Any sensible teacher would see that as "nonsuccess" if not failure. We don't. Of course not. It isn't. But students endure thousands of lessons in their lifetimes because teachers can't find a way to be courageous in their teaching. Kids, I think, deserve a risky venture.

The collaboration with Martha has reacquainted me, as a teacher educator and literacy researcher, with my high school teaching self. Ideally, that self should always be integrated into my work, but practically, that self withers, in the absence of daily practice, into the shadows cast by other professional obligations. Being in a high school classroom with students on a regular basis and being able to have daily contact with a skilled teacher like Martha makes that work more relevant. This collaboration has reminded me that not only do we, as researchers, have the obligation to test our educational theory on the grounds of practice, but we should develop our theory *as* we practice. This collaboration enabled me to create the activities and approaches for teaching literary theory to high school students with particular students in mind. Maria, Tom, David, and all the other students in Martha's classes were not merely the recipients of activities I dreamed up in solitude as some kind of theoretical abstraction; the students actually became co-creators in real time of activities that made sense in their own classroom context.

Similarly, working with Martha in this way has helped me imagine possible models for teacher development, for inservices that allow teachers to be active participants rather than passive recipients of well-rehearsed and well-traveled spiels by workshop leaders. It also has humbly reminded me of the incredible power and expertise of classroom teachers, whose instincts and commitment carry them into phenomenal teaching, unaided, and without witness. While I always try to acknowledge the quality of those teachers, it is vital that I see that power for myself.

LITERARY THEORY AND TEACHER DEVELOPMENT

Martha's engagement with literary theory holds promise for the development of other teachers as well. Through active research, opportunity for reflection, collaboration, and curricular innovation, teachers not only can transform

their own disciplinary knowledge but can set the stage for wider curricular reform as well.

CHALLENGES TO TEACHER DEVELOPMENT

Horace's Compromise by Theodore Sizer (1986) has long been one of Martha's favorite books about teaching. In Horace Smith, Sizer's composite, beleaguered teacher, Martha recognizes herself. She also recognizes the conditions of teaching that not only keep teachers from teaching well but make it difficult for teachers to think of themselves as professionals who can act as powerful, autonomous, intellectual, and independent agents of student learning. Given the relentless demand of a job that just seems to become more difficult and more complicated with each passing year, teachers have little time to keep up with current theory (both educational and literary) and are often constrained by external pressures such as standardized tests, mandated curricula, parental expectations, and prevailing educational practice. Teachers frequently feel powerless and isolated and are unable to engage in professional conversations with their peers. As Cochran-Smith and Lytle (1993) note, "The isolation of teachers at all stages of their careers is well-documented, and it is clear that the daily rhythms of school provide little time for teachers to talk, reflect, and share ideas with colleagues" (p. 86).

Preoccupied with the mechanics of the school day, teachers like Martha and Horace find little time to focus on their teaching, let alone reflect on it. As Horace laments:

> Most jobs in the real world have a gap between what would be nice and what is possible. One adjusts. The tragedy for many high school teachers is that the gap is a chasm, not crossed by reasonable and judicious adjustments. Even after adroit accommodations and devastating compromises—*only five minutes per week* on the written work of each student and an average of ten minutes of planning for each fifty-odd-minute class—the task is already crushing, in reality a sixty hour work week. (Sizer, 1986, p. 20, emphasis in original)

Since the 1984 publication of *Horace's Compromise,* educational critics and observers, including Theodore Sizer himself in *Horace's Hope* and *Horace's School,* have proposed many possible directions for reforming schools and for improving the conditions under which teachers labor and develop. Among these, teacher research has emerged as a promising source of teacher development and curricular change. Through the lens of teacher research, Martha's experience carries even greater promise for teacher development.

TEACHER RESEARCH

It might be possible to make a claim that creating, instituting, and evaluating our literary theory approach constituted a kind of teacher research for Martha. Clearly, it has provided her with an opportunity to reflect on her own classroom, to create innovative curricula, to challenge some of her own assumptions about what constitutes literary knowledge, and to experiment with her own praxis. Martha's work may fall most closely into what Cochran-Smith and Lytle (1993) call conceptual research, where

> teachers connect practice to overarching concepts and show us how broad theoretical frameworks apply to particular contexts. By analyzing the patterns and discrepancies that occur, teachers use their own interpretive frameworks as practitioners to provide a truly endemic view that is different from that of an outside observer, even if that observer assumes an anthropological stance and spends considerable time in the classroom. (p. 36)

TEACHER REFLECTION

A central element of teacher research has been the role of teacher reflection in promoting professional development and improving teaching effectiveness. Martha's reflective journals, our frequent discussions about how her students are responding to our lessons on critical theory, our more formal interviews, and our regular assessments have helped Martha to deeply reflect on literature, critical theory, and the place of theory in literary study and in the lives of her students. Like theory itself, the process of reflection seems to make Martha's teaching more self-reflexive, more deliberate. Here is an excerpt from her journal that reveals the nuances of her reflection:

> I think any classic work presents possibilities for using critical lenses. In some ways it gives classics their due—why have we been reading these books for a hundred years, anyway? I reject the cynical notion that it is because we always have read/taught them. I think it is because there is a richness that appeals to each generation of readers. It may not be the same element each generation, but there continues to be something there for us. When we teach students that there are many possibilities, we formalize the ways into a work [of literature]. I think less is left to the chance that a student will intuitively pick up on issues of class, gender, psychology, author background, or whatever, and will see common themes/ideas (archetypes). Students will know what they are doing—you're teaching metacognition in a meaningful way. And

when students know that what they are doing is taking a theoretical paradigm and applying it to a text, and that in doing so they are seeing different things, and that the framework provides them with a way to organize and control the richness that wonderful books present to us, I think this is a really powerful process.

As I have worked with kids over a five-year period with this, I realize that this is not hard. It is similar to how adults and students view technology. Grownups think technology is awesome, intimidating, something to be worked on and conquered. Grownups think literary theory is theoretical, abstract, awesome, intimidating, and certainly something best left to erudite college professors. Students, on the other hand, just do it. Find a rich story, read it, slip in a couple of possibilities: What happens when we look at the women in a Fitzgerald story? Why do we read *The Great Gatsby* in American history? What is going on with East Egg and West Egg, with Mable and Tom? Have you ever been at a huge party and not even known the host? Then give the students the vocabulary: feminist theory, historical criticism, Marxist criticism, reader response. When we look through a particular literary lens, what specific things do we look for? When we think about a book in all of these ways, how multidimensional, how rich has it become? The most important thing about lenses —or a really important thing about it—is that it gives power to the student and it honors the student. If you want to be the center of the classroom, if you want to hold the bag of goodies tightly and parcel them out stingily (is that a word?), don't do this. Literary theory gives the bag of goodies to the kids, who deserve it.

In addition to providing teachers like Martha with opportunities to reflect on their practice, our collaboration also situates curricular innovation, as does teacher research, where it belongs: in the classroom, in the hands of a teacher. This location serves two important ends. First, it facilitates the development of teacher knowledge. Second, by making teachers agents of change, it encourages the kind of locally based reform that is the heart of true school reform. The next section explores how those two ends are facilitated by using literary theory in the secondary classroom.

TEACHER KNOWLEDGE

We need to develop a different theory of knowledge for teaching, a different epistemology that regards inquiry by teachers themselves as a distinctive and important way of knowing about teaching (Cochran-Smith & Lytle, 1993).

In their pioneering book about teacher research, Cochran-Smith and Lytle (1993) argue eloquently for a reconceptualization of what constitutes teacher knowledge and teacher development. They argue that previous work on teaching "often ignores teachers' roles as theorizers, interpreters, and critics of their own practice" (p. 1). By situating research in their own classrooms and by being able to reflect and report critically on student learning, teachers are able to refine their combination of subject matter knowledge with their pedagogical content knowledge (Grossman, 1990).

In *Possible Lives,* Mike Rose (1995) describes teacher knowledge this way: "A teacher must use various kinds of knowledge—knowledge of subject matter, of practice, of one's students, of relationships within the institutional confines of mass education" (p. 42).

By reading theory and enacting her understanding of that theory through practice, Martha developed her knowledge as a literature teacher in ways that far surpassed the effectiveness of any of her previous teacher training or professional development. Martha contextualized her knowledge of theory within the framework of her teaching, and that knowledge was symbiotically transformed by her practice. Martha also learned by discussing theory and reflecting on how her new knowledge about theory was enacted in her classroom. Martha's approach to reading theory and then transforming it into practice in her own classroom affirms what Bob Fecho (1993) describes in a piece of his own "conceptual research":

> What does it mean to read as a teacher? It is my belief that teachers constitute a distinctive interpretive community and that this community—particularly as it relates to the reading of educational research and theory—has clear values and standards that dominate the way teachers approach and ultimately interpret readings. . . . Thus, reading as a teacher means, most of all, reading to translate theory into practice. (pp. 266–268)

LITERARY KNOWLEDGE

One particularly important element of her teacher knowledge that has changed as a result of her experience with literary theory is that element of Martha's pedagogical content knowledge that comprises her literary knowledge. If there are now, as Gates (1992) and Graff (1995) assert, culture and canon wars that call into question some of the very assumptions about what we teach and why, then Martha has taken up her sword and shield with a whole army of adolescent allies. Literature, for Martha, is not a sacred testimony of an unexamined heritage. She is no longer a self-described broker of literary goods. As Scholes (1985) admonishes, Martha has stopped teaching

literature and has begun to help her students to study texts. She views literature itself and the production of literature more critically. Similarly, her conception of what constitutes a text has changed. She is able to view texts as cultural artifacts, and cultural artifacts as texts. She not only thinks about teaching literature differently but also thinks differently about reading literature. Her textual power is different.

TEACHER CHANGE AS KEY TO SCHOOL CHANGE

Thus far, we have illustrated how Martha's transactions with literary theory transformed her own literary perspective, her particular approach to teaching literature, and her teaching as a whole. We also have considered how Martha's experience with literary theory has altered particular aspects of her personal life. Additionally, the preceding section discussed how the integration of literary theory into the secondary literature curriculum can facilitate teacher development. There are implications for teaching beyond the immediate circle of students in Martha's class. Those implications intersect with general practice of literature instruction as well as wider considerations of school reform.

Many educational critics, from Herb Kohl to Mike Rose to Theodore Sizer to John Goodlad, concur that the transformation of teachers is requisite for the transformation of schools. Only when individual teachers like Martha transform their own classroom practice can true educational change occur. Experimentation and the willingness to risk failure are necessary parts of that change. Mike Rose notes the importance of the educational experiments of individual exemplary teachers in *Possible Lives* (1995), "Teachers experimented with ways to create a common space where meaningful work could be done. This quality of reflective experimentation, of trying new things, of tinkering and adjusting, sometimes with uneven results, sometimes failing, was part of the history of many of the classrooms in *Possible Lives*" (p. 421).

Other accounts of school reform, from Rex Brown's *Schools of Thought* (1993) to Deborah Meier's *The Power of Their Ideas* (1995), recognize the centrality of the teacher in affecting the kinds of school reform and literacy instruction our students deserve.

Martha has assumed a position of leadership at the school where she teaches. Many younger teachers regard her as a mentor and, as she generously shares her teaching materials, she encourages her junior colleagues (as well as some of her senior ones) to consider the integration of literary theory and multiple perspectives into their own classrooms. At this writing, she is the head of her department, sits on the high school curriculum council, has been the secondary language arts curriculum coordinator, is part of the

district-wide assessment team, is the Minnesota graduation standards liaison for her high school, and is part of a National Endowment for the Humanities grant designed to integrate technology and cross-disciplinary studies throughout several departments, including French, German, social studies, and language arts. Martha also has given presentations at several national conferences both for the National Council of Teachers of English and for the College Board. The circle of influence cast by Martha's teaching continues to widen.

CONCLUSION: WHY MARTHA'S THEORETICAL JOURNEY IS IMPORTANT TO ALL TEACHERS OF LITERATURE

It doesn't always take 20 years to achieve the kind of pedagogical and philosophical evolution that Martha did, but it does take time to transform practice. Bruce Pirie (1997) writes:

> I have not tried to transform myself overnight; if I had, I would have given up in frustration. We have nothing to gain by overwhelming ourselves with a condemnation of our past and with unreasonable expectations for immediate change. We have much to gain from careful thought and reflective experimentation. We and our students have growing to do. (p. 99)

Martha began teaching a quarter of a century ago, when reader response was the most radical theoretical revolution English education had seen and when the model that prevailed was the model of teaching English to pass on a mostly Eurocentric, nearly exclusively male cultural heritage. Martha's teaching was a product not only of her teacher training but the degree to which that teacher training reflected our collective moment in history.

By contrast, as we begin a new millennium, it seems perhaps more necessary to adopt a critical stance informed by theory and to encourage our students to do the same. In this contemporary context of cultural studies, in the wake of increasing attention to issues of multiculturalism and a rethinking of what counts as a discipline or even how we define culture (Boomer, 1988; Graff, 1992), what it means to be a teacher of literature has changed. The contribution of contemporary critical theory to our collective reconceptualization of our discipline is mirrored by the way in which theory can transform not only what and how we teach but our entire sense of ourselves as teachers.

Theory clearly has had a wonderful, liberating effect on Martha's teaching. She also has reclaimed her classroom as a site of her own learning and of reform of literary instruction. Cochran-Smith and Lytle (1993) put it this way:

As Freire (1971) has suggested, [teachers] are "knowing subjects," constantly learning from the process of teaching. Here we take the more radical position that learning from teaching ought to be regarded as the primary task of teacher education across the professional life span. By "learning from teaching" we mean that inquiry ought to be regarded as an integral part of the activity of teaching and as a critical basis for decisions about practice. Furthermore, we mean that classrooms and schools ought to be treated as research sites and sources of knowledge that are most effectively accessed when teachers collaboratively interrogate and enrich their theories of practice. (p. 63)

Martha's high school language arts classroom is full of possibilities, for her students and for herself. By introducing her students to several literary theories and approaches to literary interpretation, she encourages them to think about multiple meanings for the varied literary texts they read together. This multiplicity leads Martha and her students to unpredictable possibilities and challenges in their study of literature. The excitement is evident in the enthusiastic and wide-ranging nature of the classroom talk. Martha's classroom is filled with the energy that comes only when students genuinely invest in their own learning. By incorporating multiple perspectives into the study of literature, Martha has transformed the learning of the students lucky enough to enter her kite-filled classroom. Together, we believe that theory can be as enriching to other teachers and their students.

CHAPTER EIGHT

Critical Encounters: Reading the World

The relationship between the text and the world is not simply a fascinating problem for textual theory. It is, above all others, the problem that makes textual theory necessary.

—Robert Scholes, *Textual Power*

The world is like a huge novel that needs to be interpreted. It has a very broad and confusing plot with a variety of settings and many different cultures and themes.

—Jesse, Grade 11

Critical lenses are devices of interpretation. Just as they are used to interpret literature they can be used to interpret the world. When a critical lens is used in literature, in essence, it is being applied to the world. A critical lens can be used to "read" the world because there is little, if any, difference between what is real and the literature it is customarily used for.

—Carmen, Grade 12

IT'S A WARM May Friday afternoon in St. Paul, Minnesota. The fifth-hour bell has just rung at Groveland High School. The usual formation of rows in Martha's literature classroom has been abandoned in favor of clusters of desks that today are called "learning stations." Over each station is a hand-lettered sign. One station has the name "feminist" over it, another says "Marxist," another says "reader response," while another is called "historical biographical." In addition to looking different today, the classroom also sounds different: the blues of Robert Johnson, Miles Davis, Billie Holiday and Bo Diddley competes with the afternoon announcements for the students' attention—and wins.

In groups of four, the students scurry from one station to the next, one minute considering feminist readings of Bigger Thomas's violence toward women, the next reading biographical data on Richard Wright and consider-

ing its relevance to the themes of *Native Son* (see Appendix, Activity 6). As they progress from station to station, the students recall the critical theories they have discussed all year. They adroitly apply and critique each theory. Their minds seem to shift as quickly as their feet as they move from station to station, creating multiple interpretations of an often taught classic of American literature, using contemporary literary theory to guide their way.

Later, in small groups, the students consider how these critical encounters enhanced their understanding of the text. They also evaluate the relative applicability of each lens to *Native Son*. This is no cookie-cutter exercise, no one-theory-fits-all approach. Martha knows that some students will assert that certain theories do not help their reading of this novel. She welcomes the dissonance because she also knows the students will be able to explain why certain theories are more useful than others for particular texts. She welcomes the students' resistance because critical resistance has been something she wanted them to learn. She welcomes the multiple critical encounters her students had with *Native Son*. As she surveys her disorderly room, chairs askew and folders opened at each station, she is reminded of how messy and unpredictable critical encounters can be.

CRITICAL ENCOUNTERS WITH TEXTS

Students' critical encounters with literature, with the world, and with each other are at the heart of this Theory Relay. These critical encounters also form the core of this book. Through the lenses of literary theory, the students and teachers that appear in this work transformed their study of literature into theoretical odysseys marked by significant critical encounters. Rather than simply covering literature as cultural content or focusing exclusively on the skills of reading and writing, these students and teachers used the lenses of literary theories to construct multiple ways of reading texts. Together they constructed and enacted a different kind of knowing in the literature classroom. As Cochran-Smith and Lytle (1993) remind us:

> We begin with the assumption that through their interactions, teachers and students together construct classroom life and the learning opportunities that are available. Essentially teacher and students negotiate what counts as knowledge in the classroom, who can have knowledge and how knowledge can be generated, challenged, and evaluated. (p. 45)

Critical encounters with theory help students and teachers re-evaluate what counts as knowing in the literature classroom. Contemporary literary theory helps students reshape their knowledge of texts, of themselves, and of

the worlds in which both reside. In a special issue of *Theory into Practice* dedicated to the teaching of literary theory in the high school classroom, Meredith Cherland and Jim Greenlaw (1998) remind teachers of the importance of teaching with theory:

> High school English teachers are under pressure to teach their students to read literature in ways that lead to more flexible formulations of meaning, in ways that are more relevant to their contemporary lives. . . . New forms of literary theory have useful applications in high school English classrooms and they support effective teaching practices in three different ways. First, literary theory has implications for *how people read*. Secondly, literary theory has implications for *what is read*. Thirdly, literary theory simulates the production of ideas and *discourages reductive thinking*. (p. 175, emphasis in original)

In her introduction to *Critical Theory Today: A User-Friendly Guide*, Lois Tyson (1999) summarizes the importance of studying theory and how that study transforms what we mean by knowledge:

> For knowledge isn't just something we acquire; it's something we are or hope to become. Knowledge is what constitutes our relationship to ourselves and to our world, for it is the lens through which we view ourselves and our world. Change the lens and you change both the view and the viewer. This principle is what makes knowledge at once so frightening and so liberating, so painful and so utterly, utterly joyful. (p. 11)

Jack Thomson (1993) views contemporary literary theory as a way of helping students control texts, as a way of redistributing the interpretive power in the classroom:

> Too often our students see literary criticism as the practice of subordinating their human, ethical, and political reactions to some ideal of literary value. I think we have a responsibility to help them unravel and evaluate the themes and ideologies of texts they read rather than see them as some divine or secular authority. (p. 136)

Although many of the adolescents in the classes featured in this book were initially skeptical and viewed the lenses as simply another kind of analytical tool for finding the often predetermined, singular "hidden meaning" in literature, they eventually integrated the theories into their own interpretive repertoire and registered appreciative insights about the impact of theory on their literary understanding. Following are excerpts from the reading journals of several students who confirm that, for them, reading with theory created significant and meaningful critical encounters with texts. The students'

own words demonstrate how theory became powerfully and positively integrated into their study of literature.

> Pieces of literature may convey several different meanings. Most works do, but finding the meaning can be very difficult with nowhere to start. Critical lenses give this start. Critical lenses view literature from different aspects and give meaning never thought of before to help the reader come to conclusions about a book.

> Literary theory enables a reader to be able to help pull out certain meaning and themes the authors explicitly or implicitly weave into their work.

> Critical lenses give opportunity to view literature in ways never thought of before and broaden the reader a little more for having opened up and seen things in a different light. The lenses make the reader think.

> Each piece of quality literature you read is filled with different ideas and meanings; depending on which type of lens you choose to look through, you get a different meaning out of the work.

> Lenses have helped because they are almost always recognizable in texts. It's amazing what a deeper level of understanding one can accomplish initially with lenses. They cause questioning and even hesitance towards themes and structures.

> Literary theories are used to find different meanings in a text that would not normally be seen.

> Anyone is better for having read a book and taken something away from it, but even better for looking at life through a new perspective and wanting to experience whole new events.

CRITICAL ENCOUNTERS: THE IMPORTANCE
OF MULTIPLE PERSPECTIVES

Critical lenses are about looking into elements of the world in different ways, thinking about things from different perspectives. This will never be a bad thing, no matter what [they are] used to view. . . . Seeing many different sides of stories only benefits everyone/thing.

—Joelle, Grade 11

Multiplicity, or the ability to see "many different sides of stories," as Joelle puts it, is central to the idea of teaching literary theory to adolescents. Students' ability to read texts, the world, and their own lives is enhanced not only by the study of individual theories themselves but by the notion of multiple perspectives. In his impressive argument for using literary theory to read adolescent novels, John Moore (1997) quotes Henry Louis Gates, Jr.'s apt metaphor for theory as a prism, one that changes the entire nature of what is viewed when we view it through a different angle of the prism:

> Literary theory functioned in my education as a prism, which I could turn to refract different spectral patterns of language use in a text, as one does daylight. turn the prism this way, and one pattern emerges; turn it that way, and another pattern configures. (p. 187)

By viewing individual texts through the prisms of varied theories, students were able to construct multiple perspectives. Moore also underscores the importance of literary theory in helping students learn to construct and sustain a plurality of perspectives. He argues:

> We can help our students understand what it means to read literature differently if we value multiple readings (or interpretations) over a single authoritative reading. Literary theory helps us understand that there are many ways to know texts, to read and interpret them, but many secondary school teachers are unfamiliar with the changes that have occurred in literary theory over the last four decades. (1997, p. 4)

This book is intended not only to provide teachers with the tools they need to become more familiar with contemporary literary theory, but also to emphasize the value of multiple perspectives yielded by multiple readings of texts. As I argued in Chapter 2, the ultimate pedagogical goal of teaching with theory is to facilitate students' ability to understand different perspectives. To that end, I encourage teachers to use several different critical theories with individual literary texts. With high school teachers and their students, I have developed variations on the kind of Theory Relay that was described at the beginning of this chapter (see Appendix, Activities 14 and 15 for Theory Relays on *The Things They Carried* and *Frankenstein*). These relays help students consider different critical interpretations side by side. In doing so, they become flexible thinkers and skilled interpreters, and are able to see, as Bonnycastle (1996) reminds us, that the problem of approaches to literature is really "a problem of ideologies" (p. 32).

Students' journal entries reflect their understanding of not only the im-

portance of multiple perspectives, but their ability to acknowledge and sustain them.

Every person sees things a little differently, through different eyes, and while it is not unusual for different people to look at the same thing differently, sometimes the same person can also look from different perspectives. The latter is aided by the use of critical lenses which help a reader to focus on different issues in the same book.

Lenses help readers to understand texts from different perspectives. This is so helpful because instead of having just one take on a work, the reader may have three or four. Not only does this allow the reader to see works differently, but [it] enhances the reader's understanding of the text.

Critical lenses allow us to look at something in different ways to understand what is taking place around us. If people look at things in different ways, it is possible to see the intent of other people and, in turn, [to] understand them.

How can one know who is right and who is wrong? There may never be an answer to that question, but there is a way to increase knowledge so that one may grow closer to the truth. The way to do that is to keep an open mind, look at things from different angles and then make an educated analysis.

Using different lenses helps important and diverse themes come to light.

Each piece of quality literature you read is filled with different ideas and meanings; depending on which type of lens you choose to look through, you get a different meaning out of the work.

It is sometimes difficult to grasp the meaning of a work through one's own eyes. One's experiences in life greatly influence the way one views the world around him; this most likely limits one's understanding of a piece of literature. Literary theories or critical lenses are tools that will open up many windows in one's understanding of a book. They make the reader take on a different personality, with different views of society and [oneself], thus leading to a better, wider, clearer understanding of a work.

CRITICAL ENCOUNTERS: READING WORLDS

Critical encounters with literary theory also help students to read the world around them. Teachers hope that students will be able to integrate successful strategies for learning in school and to adapt those strategies to life as well. As argued in Chapter 1, students need to learn to read the world around them in order to function as literate participants in an increasingly complex society. Jack Thomson (1993) has written, "All our regular institutional and social practices, including our social rituals and ceremonies, are texts to be read and interpreted" (p. 130).

Learning to read the world as text is an important result of high school literature instruction that includes theory. In a culminating activity called Critical Encounters: Reading the World (see Appendix, Activity 16), I asked students to bring in both artifacts and examples of personal experiences to see if they could use the lenses of literary theory to shed light on these artifacts and experiences. Here are some items students brought in for cultural analysis:

- *Time* article about teenage rage
- a television remote control
- a variety of magazine ads, generally using beautiful, young, thin women to sell everything from toothpaste to milk
- videotape of a *Jerry Springer Show*
- *People Magazine* edition featuring "the 50 most beautiful people in the world"
- body piercing and tattoos (in some cases they offered up themselves)
- credit card ads
- military recruitment posters
- photographs of a suggestive billboard for a "shock jock" radio program
- college viewbooks

In addition to these articles, students also shared particular individual experiences for cultural analysis, including some of the following:

- quitting a part-time job because of perceived sexual harassment
- a misunderstanding between two friends because someone couldn't inhabit the other person's perspective
- watching television and understanding for the first time how certain groups of people are targeted
- overhearing two male friends discussing how women can't be sportscasters because they are not good at it

- fighting with a sibling over the car
- observing at a recent school banquet that all the students who were being honored were sitting in the back talking during the entire presentation
- listening to gossip and wondering why we do it
- homecoming
- making college decisions, thinking about the future

In groups and as whole classes, the students described how they used particular literary theories to understand these artifacts and incidents. Students offered analyses that were frequently acutely feminist, Marxist, or reader response. They noticed, for example, dominant pink and red in print advertisements for sugar substitutes and described how women were visually drawn into the page. They scanned the *New York Times* and noticed the juxtaposition of ads for Cartier watches and luxury cars with articles about the endless cycle of poverty in our cities. They discussed the power structure of high school, including how power is enacted within their own relationships. After these discussions, I directly asked these students, "Can we use critical lenses to read the world?" Here are a few of their written responses:

Yes—the things we analyze in books and poems are life experiences, situations. So why not analyze real life situations? It works. Our lives are the plot, ourselves and the people we know are the characters. I say give it a shot!

I think that critical lenses are formed by the world, so they can be used to read the world.

Yes, if you keep an open mind. Using a single lens can encourage some single-mindedness, but using them all can open new dimensions.

Yes, we do this every day. The phrase "step into someone else's shoes" applies here. Whenever we try to think what someone else is feeling, you are using a lens.

Yes, because everything happens for a reason and to better understand these reasons, we need a way to read them and understand them at a deeper level. There is something inside everyone that makes them act, whether it be their feminist side or their Marxist side that we want to and need to understand.

Yes, critical lenses are devices of interpretation. Just as they are used to interpret literature, they can be used to interpret the world. The psychoanalytic lens can be used to look at a person's thoughts and motives

for action in situations. Historical lenses help us study the past and apply it to the present. People almost always think of something in their own terms like reader-response lens. A book is only a collection of situations and thoughts which are possible in real life. When a critical lens is used in literature, in essence it is being applied to the world. A critical lens can be used to "read" the world because there is little, if any, difference between what is and the literature it is customarily used for.

I believe we can use critical lenses to read the world. If we read the world through a historical lens, we begin to understand why we need so much technology and what it does for us. If we read the world through reader response, we begin to realize how important it is to have our own opinion. Without individual ideas, the world would be a very boring place. The world is like a huge novel that needs to be interpreted. It has a very broad and confusing plot with a variety of settings and many different cultures and themes.

No, we can't read the world. But we can view the world from different points of view that help us see more sides of the story.

Of course, we do it every day, or at least I do. Watching the news, for example, I saw the story about a woman in the military being court marshaled for adultery. One can look at this through a multitude of lenses. Through the eyes of the military: It must keep its members obeying orders above all else, and she lied. Feminist: It's a witch hunt, military men asserting their power. Morality: This should have never happened in the first place. Society: How come the military is held accountable for things civilians are not held liable for?

No, even when we try to understand critical lenses our understanding is filtered through our own "perspectives" or "lenses." No intellectual theory has ever truly led scholars to understand the world. We can each use our individual understandings or critical lenses to add even more variety to our many thoughts about the world, but these learned perspectives will never come near replacing our natural ones.

Yes, this would benefit the world because it would force people to understand different points of view.

Most definitely. We can look at class structure, how current historical events affect our lives, and how we feel about things that affect us. All the lenses can be applied because literature is about life and how we live it.

Yes, each day humans use these lenses to look at the world, often times we just don't have a name for them. For example, the deconstruction lens. People are always observing things and challenging what goes on around them. They usually just don't have a name for what they are doing.

I think it's a good idea to use different viewpoints to try and read different situations. If you take the time to look at something from any other viewpoint than the obvious, you'll get more meaning out of it.

Yes. Different events can be explained or solved by looking at different perspectives. This way one can piece together the puzzle and figure out what's going on.

Yes, we can use them in the world, and I think that's why we are taught that we've used these lenses all along. We actually have a name for it now.

CONCLUSION

The last student comment in the preceding section reminds us that when we teach theory, we are, more than anything else perhaps, naming what it is that we naturally do. We all try to construct a frame or world view to help us make sense of the seemingly disconnected events that confront us. Our place in the world is a theoried one. As Steven Lynn (1998) writes, "Whether we are aware of them or not, theories of some sort inevitably must guide our perceptions, our thinking, our behavior" (p. xii). W. Ross Winterowd, in his introduction to Sharon Crowley's (1989) book on deconstruction for teachers, makes the case even more strongly:

> Every English teacher acts on the basis of theory. Unless teaching is a random series of lessons, drills, and readings, chosen willy-nilly, the English class is guided by theories of language, literature, and pedagogy. That is, insofar as teachers choose readings and plan instruction, they are *implementing* a theory. The question, of course, is whether or not teachers understand the theory that guides their instruction. If we do not understand the theoretical context in which we function, we are powerless. (p. xiii, emphasis in original)

Both teachers and their students are powerless if, as Winterowd said, they do not understand the theoretical context in which they function. We may not be able to name our theories, nor are we always aware of how our ideologies (for that is what they are) become instantiated and may in fact prevent us from understanding worlds and perspectives different from our

own. We also may not be able to recognize an oppressive ideology when we are confronted with one, whether it's in a textbook, a tracking system in a high school, or in the workplace. The critical encounters encouraged by the approaches in this book will help us name our theories and consider multiple perspectives as we find our place in the texts we read and the lives we lead.

Classroom Activities

ACTIVITY 1

"Little Miss Muffet," by Russell Baker

Little Miss Muffet

By Russell Baker

Little Miss Muffet, as everyone knows, sat on a tuffet eating her curds and whey when along came a spider who sat down beside her and frightened Miss Muffet away. While everyone knows this, the significance of the event had never been analyzed until a conference of thinkers recently brought their special insights to bear upon it. Following are excerpts from the transcript of their discussion:

Sociologist: We are clearly dealing here with a prototypical illustration of a highly tensile social structure's tendency to dis- or perhaps even de-structure itself under the pressures created when optimum minimums do not obtain among the disadvantaged. Miss Muffet is nutritionally underprivileged, as evidenced by the subliminal diet of curds and whey upon which she is forced to subsist, while the spider's cultural disadvantage is evidenced by such phenomena as legs exceeding standard norms, odd mating habits, and so forth.

In this instance, spider expectations lead the culturally disadvantaged to assert demands to share the tuffet with the nutritionally underprivileged. Due to a communications failure, Miss Muffet assumes without evidence that the spider will not be satisfied to share her tuffet, but will also insist on eating her curds and perhaps even her whey. Thus, the failure to pre-establish selectively optimum norm structures diverts potentially optimal minimums from the expectation levels assumed to . . .

Militarist: Second-strike capability, sir! That's what was lacking. If Miss Muffet had developed a second-strike capability instead of squandering her resources on curds and whey, no spider on earth would have dared launch a first strike capable of carrying him right to the heart of her tuffet. I am confident that Miss Muffet had adequate notice from experts that she could not afford both curds and whey and, at the same time, support an early-spider-warning system. Yet curds alone were not good enough for Miss Muffet. She had to have whey, too. Tuffet security must be the first responsibility of every diner . . .

Book Reviewer: Written on several levels, this searing and sensitive exploration of the arachnid heart illuminates the agony and splendor of Jewish family life with a candor that is at once breathtaking in its simplicity and soul-shattering in its implied ambiguity. Some will doubtless be shocked to see such subjects as tuffets and whey discussed without flinching, but hereafter writers too timid to call a curd a curd will no longer . . .

Editorial Writer: Why has the government not seen fit to tell the public all it knows about the so-called curds-and-whey affair? It is not enough to suggest that this was merely a random incident involving a lonely spider and a young diner. In today's world, poised as it is on the knife edge of . . .

Psychiatrist: Little Miss Muffet is, course, neither little nor a miss. These are obviously the self she has created in her own fantasies to escape the reality that she is a gross divorcee whose superego makes it impossible for her to sustain a normal relationship with any man, symbolized by the spider, who, of course, has no existence outside her fantasies. Little Miss Muffet may, in fact, be a man with deeply repressed Oedipal impulses, who sees in the spider the father he would like to kill, and very well may some day unless he admits that what he believes to be a tuffet is, in fact, probably the dining room chandelier, and that what he thinks he is eating is, in fact, probably . . .

Student Demonstrator: Little Miss Muffet, tuffets, curds, whey, and spiders are what's wrong with education today. They're all irrelevant. Tuffets are irrelevant. Curds are irrelevant. Whey is irrelevant. Meaningful experience! How can you have relevance without meaningful experience? And how can there ever be meaningful experience without understanding? With understanding and meaningfulness and relevance, there can be love and good and deep seriousness and education today will be freed of slavery and Little Miss Muffet, and life will become meaningful and . . .

Child: This is about a little girl who gets scared by a spider.

(The child was sent home when the conference broke for lunch. It was agreed that he was too immature to subtract anything from the sum of human understanding.)

Now it's your turn to recast a familiar fairy tale or Mother Goose rhyme from at least three perspectives. Work in groups of three or four and use Mr. Baker's piece as a guide.

ACTIVITY 2

Group Exercise for "Separating," by John Updike

Read the story "Separating" on your own. Then, get into groups of three or four and work together on the following questions.

1. List all the characters that appear in the story.

2. From whose point of view is the story told?

3. Summarize the story from that character's point of view. That is, according to the character you named in question 2, what happens in this story?

4. Now, pick another character from those you listed in question 1. Summarize the story from the viewpoint of that character.

5. Reread the last two paragraphs of the story. Speculate together on what will happen next. Is there any reason to believe that Richard and Joan might not separate?

6. Extend the story. Write at least one page *from the point of view of the character you used in question 4.*

ACTIVITY 3

Theory Wars: Looking at *Star Wars* Through Critical Lenses

In your groups, discuss the following questions. You will be asked to share the fruits of your discussion with the whole class in your symposium.

1. Try to recall the first time you saw this film. In what ways was this view-ing different from your first viewing. What were some things you noticed that you didn't notice before? What seemed to be important this time that didn't come through in a previous viewing?

2. Think back to our discussions of archetypes from last year. Describe how characters, plot, conflict, or theme in *Star Wars* could be viewed in arche-typal terms. For example, is this a classic story of good versus evil, is Princess Leia the typical heroine?

3. Read through the definitions of the literary theories (see Activity 4). Select the two theories that you think might be most helpful in illuminating the film. Write down the theories below.

    1. _____ 2. _____

4. Now come up with some statements about the film for each of the theories you named in question 3. For example, if you selected feminist criticism you might discuss the lack of female characters and evaluate the role of Princess Leia from a feminist perspective. If you chose reader-response the-ory you might describe how the film reminded you of a personal experience in your struggle with good and evil. (Use loose-leaf paper—journal potential).

5. After you discuss these interpretations, decide how to present them to the whole class. Your presentation should be no more than about 10 minutes of your symposium.

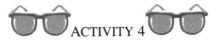

Literary Theories: A Sampling of Critical Lenses

Literary theories were developed as a means to understand the various ways people read texts. The proponents of each theory believe their theory is *the* theory, but most of us interpret texts according to the "rules" of several different theories at a time. All literary theories are lenses through which we can see texts. There is nothing to say that one is better than another or that you should read according to any of them, but it is sometimes fun to "decide" to read a text with one in mind because you often end up with a whole new perspective on your reading.

What follows is a summary of some of the most common schools of literary theory. These descriptions are extremely cursory, and none of them fully explains what the theory is all about. But it is enough to get the general idea. Enjoy!

Archetypal Criticism. In criticism, "archetype" signifies narrative designs, character types, or images that are said to be identifiable in a wide variety of works of literature, as well as in myths, dreams, and even ritualized modes of social behavior. The archetypal similarities within these diverse phenomena are held to reflect a set of universal, primitive, and elemental patterns, whose effective embodiment in a literary work evokes a profound response from the reader. The death-rebirth theme is often said to be the archetype of archetypes. Other archetypal themes are the journey underground, the heavenly ascent, the search for the father, the paradise–Hades image, the Promethean rebel-hero, the scapegoat, the earth goddess, and the fatal woman.

Feminist Criticism. A feminist critic sees cultural and economic disabilities in a "patriarchal" society that have hindered or prevented women from realizing their creative possibilities and women's cultural identification as a merely negative object, or "Other," to man as the defining and dominating "Subject." There are several assumptions and concepts held in common by most feminist critics.

1. Our civilization is pervasively patriarchal.
2. The concepts of "gender" are largely, if not entirely, cultural constructs, effected by the omnipresent patriarchal biases of our civilization.
3. This patriarchal ideology also pervades those writings that have been considered great literature. Such works lack autonomous female role models, are implicitly addressed to male readers, and leave the woman reader an alien outsider or else solicit her to identify against herself by assuming male values and ways of perceiving, feeling, and acting.

This is somewhat like Marxist criticism, but instead of focusing on the relationships between the classes it focuses on the relationships between the genders. Under this theory you would examine the patterns of thought, behavior,

values, enfranchisement, and power in relations between the sexes. For example, "Where Are You Going, Where Have You Been" can be seen as the story of the malicious dominance men have over women both physically and psychologically. Connie is the female victim of the role in society that she perceives herself playing—the coy young lass whose life depends on her looks.

Marxist Criticism. A Marxist critic grounds theory and practice on the economic and cultural theory of Karl Marx and Friedrich Engels, especially on the following claims:

1. The evolving history of humanity, its institutions and its ways of thinking are determined by the changing mode of its "material production"—that is, of its basic economic organization.
2. Historical changes in the fundamental mode of production effect essential changes both in the constitution and power relations of social classes, which carry on a conflict for economic, political, and social advantage.
3. Human consciousness in any era is constituted by an ideology—that is, a set of concepts, beliefs, values, and ways of thinking and feeling through which human beings perceive, and by which they explain, what they take to be reality. A Marxist critic typically undertakes to "explain" the literature in any era by revealing the economic, class, and ideological determinants of the way an author writes, and to examine the relation of the text to the social reality of that time and place.

This school of critical theory focuses on power and money in works of literature. Who has the power/money? Who does not? What happens as a result? For example, it could be said that "The Legend of Sleepy Hollow" is about the upper class attempting to maintain their power and influence over the lower class by chasing Ichabod, a lower-class citizen with aspirations toward the upper class, out of town. This would explain some of the numerous descriptions of land, wealth, and hearty living through Ichabod's eyes.

New Criticism is directed against the prevailing concern of critics with the lives and psychology of authors, with social background, and with literary history. There are several points of view and procedures that are held in common by most New Critics.

1. A poem should be treated as primarily poetry and should be regarded as an independent and self-sufficient object.
2. The distinctive procedure of the New Critic is explication, or close reading: The detailed and subtle analysis of the complex interrelations and ambiguities of the components within a work.
3. The principles of New Criticism are basically verbal. That is, literature is conceived to be a special kind of language whose attributes are defined by systematic opposition to the language of science and of practical and logical discourse. The key concepts of this criticism deal

with the meanings and interactions of words, figures of speech, and symbols.
4. The distinction between literary genres is not essential.

Psychological and Psychoanalytic Criticism. Psychological criticism deals with a work of literature primarily as an expression, in fictional form, of the personality, state of mind, feelings, and desires of its author. The assumption of psychoanalytic critics is that a work of literature is correlated with its author's mental traits.

1. Reference to the author's personality is used to explain and interpret a literary work.
2. Reference to literary works is made in order to establish, biographically, the personality of the author.
3. The mode of reading a literary work itself is a way of experiencing the distinctive subjectivity or consciousness of its author.

This theory requires that we investigate the psychology of a character or an author to figure out the meaning of a text (although to apply an author's psychology to a text can also be considered biographical criticism, depending on your point of view). For example, alcohol allows the latent thoughts and desires of the narrator of "The Black Cat" to surface in such a way that he ends up shirking the self-control imposed by social mores and standards and becomes the man his psyche has repressed his whole life.

Reader-Response Criticism. This type of criticism does not designate any one critical theory, but focuses on the activity of reading a work of literature. Reader-response critics turn from the traditional conception of a work as an achieved structure of meanings to the responses of readers as their eyes follow a text. By this shift of perspective a literary work is converted into an activity that goes on in a reader's mind, and what had been features of the work itself—including narrator, plot, characters, style, and structure—are less important than the connection between a reader's experience and the text. It is through this interaction that meaning is made.

This is the school of thought most students seem to adhere to. Proponents believe that literature has no objective meaning or existence. People bring their own thoughts, moods, and experiences to whatever text they are reading and get out of it whatever they happen to, based on their own expectations and ideas. For example, when I read "Sonny's Blues" I am reminded of my younger sister who loves music. The story really gets to me because sometimes I worry about her and my relationship with her. I want to support her in a way that Sonny's brother does not support Sonny.

Other theories we'll be discussing in class include:

Deconstruction. Deconstruction is, by far, the most difficult critical theory for people to understand. It was developed by some very smart (or very unstable)

people who declare that literature means nothing because language means nothing. In other words, we cannot say that we know what the "meaning" of a story is because there is no way of knowing. For example, in some stories (like "Where Are You Going, Where Have You Been") that do not have tidy endings, you cannot assume you know what happened.

Historical Criticism. Using this theory requires that you apply to a text specific historical information about the time during which an author wrote. History, in this case, refers to the social, political, economic, cultural, and/or intellectual climate of the time. For example, William Faulkner wrote many of his novels and stories during and after World War II, which helps to explain the feelings of darkness, defeat, and struggle that pervade much of his work.

Structuralism. This is different from structural criticism, which looks at the "universal" qualities of a piece of literature. Structuralism is a theory that concentrates completely on the text, bringing nothing else to it. It depends, in large part, on linguistic theory, so it is difficult to do without some background. On the very most basic level, however, structuralism investigates the kinds of patterns that are built up and broken down within a text and uses them to get at an interpretation of that text. For example, in *Our Town* each act begins with the Stage Manager providing factual information, moves toward the introduction of a "standard" concern in life, makes that concern seem insignificant, and then uses a character to comment on, or moralize on, that concern. This pattern indicates that the play is not actually the slow movement through the lives of some standard characters but a satire of the basic and ridiculous things humans consistently concern themselves with.

ACTIVITY 5

Reader Response and *Running Fiercely*

Context
(What factors surrounding my reading of
the text are influencing my response?)

Reader (your name) ———▶ Meaning ◀——— Text (*Running Fiercely*)

(What personal qualities, or events
relevant to this particular book,
might influence my response?)

(What textual features might
influence my response?)

ACTIVITY 6

Theory Relay: *Native Son*

For the next hour in groups of three or four, please consider *Native Son* from a variety of theoretical perspectives: historical/biographical, reader response, Marxist, and feminist. We'll be doing this as a kind of relay. There are four theory stations around the room. Spend approximately 10 minutes at each station. Each person should turn in one of these sheets to the teacher. Make certain you've completed the journal entry at the end of the sheet.

Name:

Group Members:

Reader-Response Station
Reread the explanation of reader response and study your reader-response diagram. In the space below, write at least three meaning statements that are the result of your personal interaction with the text.

1.

2.

3.

Historical/Biographical Station
Skim together "How Bigger Was Born" (in your copy of *Native Son*) and skim the remainder of the biographical articles that you find at this station. How does what you've learned, as well as any additional experience or reading you've had with other works of Richard Wright, affect and inform your understanding of *Native Son?*

Feminist Station
Consider the quotation you find at the feminist station. As a group, construct an interpretation of the quotation that is informed by your collective understanding of feminist literary theory. When you consider *Native Son* from a feminist perspective, what characters, incidents, or themes are brought into greater relief? Write your response below.

Marxist Station
Consider the quotation you find at the Marxist station. As a group, construct an interpretation of the quotation that is informed by your understanding of Marxist literary theory. When you consider *Native Son* from a Marxist perspective, what characters, incidents, or themes are brought into greater relief? Write your response below.

Journal Entry:
Reflect on your group's efforts this hour to read *Native Son* through a variety of critical lenses. Which lens seemed to be most consistent with the intention of the novel? Which lens was the most difficult to apply? Which was the most informative? (This entry should be at least two full paragraphs. Write it on a separate piece of paper that you attach to this sheet.)

ACTIVITY 7

Reader Response and *Native Son*

Context
(What factors surrounding my reading of
the text are influencing my response?)

Reader (your name) ——————▶ Meaning ◀—————— Text (*Native Son*)

(What personal qualities, or
events relevant to this particular
book, might influence my
response?)

(What textual features
might influence my
response?)

ACTIVITY 8

Key Ideas of Marx

Stages of History

Marx believed that history moved in stages: from feudalism to capitalism, socialism, and ultimately communism.

Materialism

Each stage was mainly shaped by the economic system. The key to understanding the systems was to focus on the "mode of production." (For example, most production under feudalism was agricultural, while most production under capitalism was industrial). It also was necessary to focus on who owned the "means of production." (Under capitalism, a small class—the bourgeoisie—owned the factories. Under socialism, the factories would be owned by the workers.)

Class Struggle

"The history of all hitherto existing society is the history of class struggles." Each system, up to and including capitalism, was characterized by the exploitation of one class by another.

The Dialectic

Marx believed that great historical changes followed a three-step pattern called thesis–antithesis–synthesis. Any idea or condition (thesis) brought into being its opposite (antithesis). For example, the existence of the ruling bourgeoisie under capitalism made necessary the existence of its opposite, the proletariat. The two opposites would conflict until they produced a new, higher stage (synthesis).

Internal Contradictions

Each class system therefore contained the seeds of its own destruction, which Marx sometimes called "internal contradictions." Capitalism, he believed, was

plagued by such contradictions, which would get worse and worse until they destroyed it.

Capitalism

Marx saw capitalism as the cruelest, most efficient system yet evolved for the exploitation of the working majority by a small class of owners. It was the nature of capitalism, Marx believed, for wealth and ownership to be concentrated into an ever-shrinking class of mega-rich. This was one of many internal contradictions of capitalism that would inevitably destroy it.

Working-Class Misery

It was the nature of capitalist production methods to become more and more technologically efficient, requiring fewer and fewer workers to produce more and more goods. Therefore, capitalism would be plagued by bouts of high unemployment. As machines made a worker's skill less important, wages would be pushed ever downward. As each worker became simply an appendage of a machine, his or her job would be less satisfying, and the worker would become more alienated.

Class Consciousness

Such total exploitation of so many by so few could not last forever. The workers would inevitably develop "class consciousness," or an awareness of their predicament. When that occurred, it would be fairly simple to take over the factories and the state.

End of History

Since class conflict was the engine that drove history, and since under communism there would be no class distinctions, history would come to its final resting place in a system free of exploitation.

ACTIVITY 9

Reading *Hamlet* Through the Marxist Lens

Act 1—Warm-Up Discussion

First things first. This stuff can be pretty cool but takes a bit of practice. It can be hard, but I've heard you're pretty smart readers. So here goes. Have you considered Marxist literary theory in your reading before? With what texts? How did that consideration affect your reading of the text as a whole?

The article you read, "Marxist Criticism" by Stephen Bonnycastle, states that in order to understand *Hamlet* from a Marxist perspective, you need to know something about Shakespeare's times and the class struggle present then. What *do* you know about that?

An *ideology* is a view of the world, a prevailing set of beliefs. What are some examples of ideologies you have come across?

What is the prevailing ideology that is represented in *Hamlet?* Are there other differing views of the world that fight with one another within the text? Explain.

Act 2—In Trios and Then as a Class

"Marxist criticism pays a lot of attention to the social structures that allocate power to different groups in society." List some of the social groups that are represented in *Hamlet*.

We've all heard the term "social ladder." Try plotting some of the characters on the social ladder graph below.

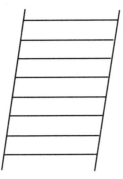

Name some of the primary power struggles that the play portrays. Who has the power and who doesn't?

Conflict between:

Has Power	Has No Power

Put a * next to the power struggles that could be considered class conflicts.

Act 3—On Your Own

The following questions should be done on your own. You don't have to share your responses to the first one, but we may discuss your responses to the second and third questions in class tomorrow.

Marxist literary theory asserts the importance of paying attention to class conflicts, power struggles, and how we place ourselves within the particular social structure in which we find ourselves. Draw a picture or diagram, if you can, of the existing power or class structure in which you live. You can do it like the

social ladder used above, or you can draw concentric circles, or you can map or web; anything is fine. Where are you, relative to where power and money is located?

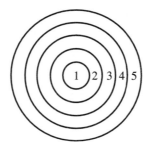

To what degree do you think this location may have affected your reading of *Hamlet*? What characters in *Hamlet* do you feel most closely represent where you are socially?

Marxist literary theory encourages us to look at the big political questions that surround our more personal concerns. List below some of the big questions that emerge for you as a result of reading *Hamlet* through a Marxist lens.

Now think of one or two smaller, more personal and perhaps more important questions that emerge for you as you think about issues of class conflict, ideologies or beliefs, and struggle. List them below.

ACTIVITY 10

Through Rose-Colored Glasses: The Feminist Lens

1. What is feminism?

2. What is feminist literary theory?

3. Try to interpret this concrete poem in two ways, from a traditional perspective and from a feminist perspective:

—Pedro Xisto

4. Can the feminist lens be useful in everyday life? Please write a sentence about the following objects or situations using a traditional perspective and then applying the feminist lens:

    •   Mount Rushmore

    •   the Miss America pageant

    •   coverage of the Olympic women's hockey team

    •   the sex scandal in the White House

    •   anchors of national network news shows

    •   Madonna's lingerie

5. Can you think of anything that has happened to you or to a friend of yours in the past 2 weeks that could be better explained or understood through a feminist lens? Pick a partner and share stories.

ACTIVITY 11

What Color Are Your Walls? The Feminist Lens

1. What is the feminist lens?

Feminist literary criticism helps us look at literature in a different light. It applies the philosophies and perspectives of feminism to the literature we read. There are many different kinds of feminist literary theory. Some theorists examine the language and symbols that are used and how that language and use of symbols are "gendered." Others remind us that men and women write differently, and analyze how the gender of the author affects how literature is written. Many feminist critics look at how the characters, especially the female characters, are portrayed and ask us to consider how the portrayal of female characters "reinforces or undermines" sexual stereotypes (Lynn, 1998). Feminist literary theory also suggests that the gender of the reader often affects our response to a text. For example, feminist critics may claim that certain male writers address their readers as if they were all men and exclude the female reader.

Like feminism itself, feminist literary theory asks us to consider the relationships between men and women and their relative roles in society. Much feminist literary theory reminds us that the relationship between men and women in society is often unequal and reflects a particular patriarchal ideology. Those unequal relationships may appear in a variety of ways in the production of literature and within literary texts. Feminist theorists invite us to pay particular attention to the patterns of thought, behavior, values, and power in those relationships.

Feminist literary critics remind us that literary values, conventions, and even the production of literature have themselves been historically shaped by men. They invite us to consider writings by women, both new and forgotten, and also ask us to consider viewing familiar literature through a feminist perspective.

2. Consider Gertrude and Ophelia from *Hamlet.*

For each character, write two descriptive statements—one from a "traditional" masculine perspective and the second from a feminist perspective.

Gertrude:

Traditional statement:

Feminist statement:

Ophelia:

Traditional statement:

Feminist statement:

3. How do we apply the feminist lens?

We apply it by closely examining the portrayal of the characters, both female and male, the language of the text, the attitude of the author, and the relationship between the characters. We also consider the comments the author seems to be making about society as a whole. Let's try to interpret the following concrete poem in two ways, from a traditional perspective and from a feminist perspective:

 —Pedro Xisto

4. Now, think about "The Yellow Wallpaper."

Using the feminist lens, write a brief analysis of the narrator, her situation, and perhaps Perkins Gilman's intent in writing the piece. Consider Perkins Gilman's audience as well. Finally, what meaning(s) did you derive from the text as you applied the feminist lens? (Note: this is very similar to the kind of analysis you may be asked to do in a college English class.)

ACTIVITY 12

A Lens of One's Own:
Using Feminist Literary Theory

1. What is the feminist lens?

Feminist literary criticism helps us look at literature in a different light. It applies the philosophies and perspectives of feminism to the literature we read. There are many different kinds of feminist literary theory. Some theorists examine the language and symbols that are used and how that language and use of symbols are "gendered." Others remind us that men and women write differently and analyze how the gender of the author affects how literature is written. Many feminist critics look at how the characters, especially the female characters, are portrayed and ask us to consider how the portrayal of female characters "reinforces or undermines" sexual stereotypes (Lynn, 1998). Feminist literary theory also suggests that the gender of the reader often affects our response to a text. For example, feminist critics may claim that certain male writers address their readers as if they were all men and exclude the female reader.

Like feminism itself, feminist literary theory asks us to consider the relationships between men and women and their relative roles in society. Much feminist literary theory reminds us that the relationship between men and women in society is often unequal and reflects a particular patriarchal ideology. Those unequal relationships may appear in a variety of ways in the production of literature and within literary texts. Feminist theorists invite us to pay particular attention to the patterns of thought, behavior, values, and power in those relationships.

Feminist literary critics remind us that literary values, conventions, and even the production of literature have themselves been historically shaped by men. They invite us to consider writings by women, both new and forgotten, and also ask us to consider viewing familiar literature through a feminist perspective.

2. How do we apply the feminist lens?

We apply it by closely examining the portrayal of the characters, both female and male, the language of the text, the attitude of the author, and the relationship between the characters. We also consider the comments the author seems to be making about society as a whole.

3. Is Virginia Woolf a feminist?

In groups of two or three, state whether the feminist literary lens would meet with Virginia Woolf's approval. Does she agree that our readings are "gendered"? Does she believe that women characters and writers "get the shaft"? Be prepared

to defend your statement with at least two quotations from *A Room of One's Own.*

Our position is:

Quotation 1:

Quotation 2:

4. Application: Looking through the feminist lens

Select two female characters from novels with which you are very familiar. They could be from our summer reading, from works we have read together, or from texts you have read in previous English classes. For example, you might choose Daisy from *The Great Gatsby,* Hester Prynne from *The Scarlet Letter,* Sonya from *Crime and Punishment,* etc.

For each character, write two descriptive statements—one from a traditional masculine perspective and the second from a feminist perspective.

Character 1:

Traditional statement:

Feminist statement:

Character 2:

Traditional statement:

Feminist statement:

ACTIVITY 13

Deconstruction

Deconstruction is, by far, the most difficult critical lens for people to understand. It is an intellectually sophisticated theory that confuses many very smart people, but we think so much of you, that we know you can understand it. It is a postmodern theory, and like most postmodernism, it questions many of the basic assumptions that have guided us in the past. In the traditional study of literature, those basic assumptions include:

- Language is stable and has meaning we can all agree on.
- The author is in control of the text s/he writes.
- Works of literature have an internal consistency.
- Works of literature have an external relevance.
- You can take the author's or poet's word for what s/he writes.
- There is a set of interpretive tools that you can reliably use to interpret a literary text.

Deconstruction calls all of these assumptions into question. It asks you to read resistantly, to not take a work of literature at its face value, and to question the assumptions, both literary and philosophical, that the work or the author asks you to make. It is this kind of resistance that you folks are so good at. And it is that resistance, that ability to look beyond what seems to be intended, that will be a useful skill in the "real world." It helps us to become careful and skeptical consumers of culture, not passive recipients of "great works."

Deconstructionist critics ask us to probe beyond the surface or recognizable constructs of a finished story or text. By "construct," we mean something that has been constructed by mental synthesis. That is, constructs are created when we combine things we know through our senses or from our experiences. They do not exist naturally; they are products of our intervention into the order of the universe. When we re-examine and challenge the constructs employed by the literary writer, we "deconstruct." The term does NOT simply mean to take it apart. It means we need to look thoughtfully beyond the surface of the text—"to peel away like an onion the layers of constructed meanings." It doesn't mean the same thing as analyzing. In the traditional sense, when we *analyze* a piece, we put it back the way it was and appreciate it more. When we *deconstruct* a piece of literature, we realize that there is something wrong or incomplete or dishonest or unintended with how it was put together in the first place.

Here is one good explanation of deconstruction:

"Having been written by a human being with unresolved conflicts and contradictory emotions, a story may disguise rather than reveal the underlying anxieties or perplexities of the author. Below the surface, unresolved tensions or contradictions may account for the true dynamics of the story. The story may have one message for the ordinary unsophisticated reader and another for the reader who responds to its subtext, its subsurface ironies. Readers who deconstruct a text will be 'resistant' readers. They will not be taken in by what a story says on the surface but will try to penetrate the disguises of the text. . . . They may engage in radical rereading of familiar classics" (Guth & Rico, 1996, p. 366).

Here is another useful definition:

"Deconstruction is a strategy for revealing the underlayers of meaning in a text that were suppressed or assumed in order for it to take its actual form. . . . Texts are never simply unitary but include resources that run counter to their assertions and/or their authors' intentions" (Appignanesi & Garratt, 1999, p. 80).

We're going to play with deconstruction today in three steps: first with some common metaphors, then with a traditional poem, and then with some texts you've read for this class.

1. Unpacking Metaphors

Let's take some metaphors and see if there is anything false or unintended about their meaning. Under each, please write the obvious surface meaning, and an unintended meaning that may lie beneath the surface.

Love is a rose.

intended

unintended

You are the sunshine of my life.

intended

unintended

The test was a bear.

intended

unintended

2. Deconstructing a Text

Let's read the following poem, one that's often subject to traditional analysis:

Death Be Not Proud

Death be not proud, though some have called thee
Mighty and dreadful, for, thou art not so,
For those, whom thou think'st, thou dost overthrow,
Die not, poor death, nor yet canst thou kill me.
From rest and sleep, which but thy pictures be,
Much pleasure, then from thee, much more must flow,
And soonest our best men with thee do go,
Rest of their bones, and soul's delivery.
Thou art slave to fate, chance, kings, and desperate men,
And dost with poison, war, and sickness dwell,
And poppy, or charms can make us sleep as well,
And better than thy stroke; why swell'st thou then?
One short sleep past, we wake eternally,
And death shall be no more; death, thou shalt die.

                        —John Donne

What is the poem supposed to say? How would you approach it for, say, the AP exam? What traditional tools of analysis might you employ to unpack the meaning of the text?

Where does the poem break down? How might it work against the author's intentions? Write down some specific places where the text falls apart.

3. Reconsidering a Reading

Now, think of a poem, short story, or novel you've read that cannot be taken at face value, that may reveal, because of internal inconsistencies or unintended conflict and the failure of language to really communicate what we mean (even in the hands of gifted writers), a mixed message or an unintended meaning. On

your own or with a partner, please complete the following sentences about the text. We will ask you to detach this page from the handout and turn it in.

Name(s):

Text:

When I *deconstruct* this text, here's what happens. I think the main idea the author/poet was trying to construct was:

But this construct really doesn't work. The idea falls apart. The language and construction of the text aren't able to convey what the author meant to convey. There are places in the text where it just doesn't work. For example:

So, in the end, even though the author meant the work to say

it really said

(Optional) I'd also like to say that:

ACTIVITY 14

Literary Theory: Among the Things We Carry

Please consider the stories from Tim O'Brien's *The Things They Carried* from the perspective of the four theories listed below. Each group will consider a particular lens and then we will discuss this together as a whole class. Note, too, that your paper assignment is also related to this exercise. Here is a list of the stories: "The Things They Carried," "Love," "Spin," "On the Rainy River," "Enemies," "Friends," "How to Tell a True War Story," "The Dentist," "Sweetheart of the Song Tra Bong," "Stockings," "Church," "The Man I Killed," "Ambush," "Style," "Speaking of Courage," "Notes," "In the Field," "Good Form," "Field Trip," "The Ghost Soldiers," "Night Life," "The Lives of the Dead."

	Reader Response	Historical	Feminist	Marxist
Which stories lend themselves to this particular lens?				
Cite a specific textual passage or passages that support this kind of reading.				
Interpret at least one character through this lens.				
If you look through this lens, what questions emerge?				
If these stories are to be considered as a coherent whole, what is the nature of the "glue" that holds them together?				
Do you believe in this reading? Why or why not?				

ACTIVITY 15

Literary Theory: A Frankenstein Monster

Please consider Mary Shelley's *Frankenstein* in light of the following theories. Fill out as much of the chart as you can. We'll be discussing it together as a whole class.

	Reader Response	Psychoanalytic	Feminist	Marxist	Other
Citation of a specific textual passage that supports this kind of reading.					
List at least two incidents that support this kind of reading.					
Interpret at least one character through this lens.					
If you look through this lens, what themes/ issues emerge?					
What symbols do you see?					
Do you believe in this reading? Why or why not?					

ACTIVITY 16

Critical Encounters: Reading the World

Literary theory raises those issues which are often left submerged beneath the mass of information contained in the course, and it also asks questions about how the institution of great literature works. What makes a "great work" great? Who makes the decisions about what will be taught? Why are authors grouped into certain historical periods? The answers to fundamental questions like these are often unarticulated assumptions on the part of both the professor (teacher) and the students. Socrates said that the unexamined life is not worth living. . . . Literary theory is at its best when it helps us realize what we are really doing when we study literature.

—S. Bonnycastle

1. Based on our reading as well as class discussions, briefly describe in your own words the following literary theories. (Spend no more than a few minutes on this part of the exercise.)

psychological criticism

feminist literary theory

Marxism

reader-response theory

other? (Choose one as a group)

2. In groups of three or four, select a literary work with which you are all familiar. It could be a poem, a short story, a play, or a novel. Or focus on the novel you are currently using for your reader's choice. Then think of two theories that would be fruitful to use to explore that text. In the spaces

below, briefly describe how each of those two theories might be used to illuminate the text.

Theory 1:

Theory 2:

3. Now, think of something you've read, heard, or seen outside of class that particularly struck you as worth thinking about. It could be an interaction between two people, an MTV video, a song, a film or a scene from a film, a magazine article, or an ad. Briefly explain it below.

4. What lens might you use to help you understand this event or artifact? How would that lens affect or increase your understanding?

5. Can we use critical lenses to "read" the world? Explain.

6. What, if anything, do you find difficult about reading literature with critical lenses?

ACTIVITY 17

Looking Through Lenses: Our First Look

Group Members:

Summer Reading Text:

1. In three or four sentences, please summarize the plot of the book.

2. What were some of the most important things you noticed about the text before we read our discussion of lenses?

3. Which two lenses do you think might be most useful to apply to this text?

4. Which lenses do you think might not be particularly useful? Why?

5. Now try applying the two lenses that you selected in question 3.

Lens 1

When we viewed this book through the _____ lenses, we looked at:

The lenses helps us see the following things that we didn't notice before:

Therefore, we see that this might be a book about:

Lens 2

When we viewed this book through the _____ lenses, we looked at:

The lenses helps us see the following things that we didn't notice before:

Therefore, we see that this might be a book about:

Journal Entry:

Reflecting on the above, write an entry in your journal summarizing what you discovered from this activity. What worked, what went "clunk"?

What were the most and least useful elements of this first application of critical lenses?

ACTIVITY 18

Poem Analysis

Name _____

Name of poem _____ Page _____

Directions: Answer the following questions in complete sentences. You will present this to the class in an oral presentation.

1. In one sentence, what attracted you to this poem?

2. In one sentence, what made you keep reading?

3. What did you get out of this poem?

4. Put on any of the lenses you read about in the *New Yorker* article and complete the following statements:

    A. If I put this lens (_____) on for just a moment, this is what I see:

    B. If I change lenses (_____), I see this:

ACTIVITY 19

Questions and Resistance:
Closing Activity for Shorter Works

Each pair of students will look at one of the shorter works we've looked at so far from a variety of critical perspectives. Get your own thinking straight with questions 1 and 2; then put on your critical lenses one at a time and see what happens.

Title of the work:

1. In two to three sentences summarize the plot or content of the work.

2. Looking at question 1, what is this work about (think theme)?

• When putting on our *New Critical* lenses, we look at:

   We see that this is a work about:

• When putting on our *Marxist* lenses, we look at:

   We see that this is a work about:

• When putting on our *historical* lenses, we look at:

   We see that this is a work about:

• When putting on our *feminist* lenses, we look at:

   We see that this is a work about:

• When putting on our *reader-response* lenses, we look at:

   We see that this is a work about:

Reflecting on the above, write an entry in your journal summarizing what you discovered from this activity. What worked, what was strained, what went "clunk"?

ACTIVITY 20

Waking Up to *The Awakening,*
Or, What's Gender Got to Do with It?

Please divide into gender-specific groups. Then respond to the following questions:

1. What kinds of relationships between men and women are portrayed in the novel? Based on those portraits, what kinds of generalizations can we make about the relationships between men and women that we see, especially about marriage?

2. Write a few sentences about how Robert is portrayed. Think about his physical description, his behavior, his power or lack of it. What kinds of words are used to describe him? Be specific.

3. Write a few sentences about how Edna is portrayed. Think about her physical description, her behavior, her power or lack of it. What kinds of words are used to describe her? Be specific.

4. In a sentence or two, please summarize your current understanding of what it means to read a novel with a feminist lens.

5. Select a passage from what you've read so far in *The Awakening* where reading with a feminist lens proved useful or natural. Cite below the page where the passage may be found. Page #:

6. How does being a *female* or *male* affect your reading of the novel? How might the opposite sex approach this novel differently?

!!! WARNING !!!
IF YOU'VE ALREADY FINISHED THE NOVEL
OR KNOW HOW IT ENDS, PLEASE EXCUSE YOURSELF
FROM THE DISCUSSION NOW. WE MEAN IT!

7. Predict how the argument will end. Support your hypothesis with a reasonable argument as well as textual evidence.

We'll now reconvene as a whole class and compare our answers.

ACTIVITY 21

Looking Through Lenses: *Hamlet*

Names:

The lens our group will work with today is the＿＿＿＿＿＿lens.

1. In three or four sentences please summarize this lens as you understand it. What does it require the reader to consider and notice as we analyze literary texts?

2. Select one character, one scene, and one passage from *Hamlet* that seem to support the kind of reading this lens suggests. Be specific in your discussion.

Character: Reason:

Episode: Reason:

Passage: Reason:

3. Try to create a general reading of *Hamlet* from the perspective of your lens to present to the whole class. The following format might be useful:

When we viewed this book through the＿＿＿＿＿＿lens, we looked at:

This lens helps us see the following things that we didn't notice before:

Therefore, we see that this might be a play about:

4. After listening to the presentations of the other groups, please discuss the following question:

Which lens or lenses seem most helpful and relevant to our understanding of *Hamlet*? Why?

ACTIVITY 22

What Makes the *Heart of Darkness* Beat:
Looking Through a Structuralist Lens

Structuralism is yet another lens of literary theory. It means many different things to many different people and can be somewhat confusing, but it's nothing you pros can't handle! We are going to try our hand at a particular kind of structuralism, one that looks at the underlying structures of *language* as a way of understanding the underlying structures of *literature*. After all, literature is a verbal art that we can come to better understand by closely examining the word choice of skilled authors such as Joseph Conrad.

1. Arrange yourselves into five groups.
2. Look carefully at the two passages from *Heart of Darkness.*
3. Each group, using colored pens or pencils, should mark its copy of the passages in the following ways:

    Group 1: Mark all the proper nouns.
    Group 2: Mark all the verbs.
    Group 3: Mark all the adjectives.
    Group 4: Mark all the adverbs.
    Group 5: Mark sentences that seem to move the plot or narrative.

4. Now, rearrange yourselves in groups of five, so that each of the original groups is represented. Everyone should have a copy of the passages that is marked differently.
5. Look closely at the markings. Then answer the following questions:

    By looking at the nouns and adjectives, what can you say about the characters' attributes?

    By looking at the verbs and adverbs, what can you say about the characters' actions?

    By looking at the sentences, what can you say about the narrative sequence?

The Big Question:

What did you notice by looking at specific word choice that you hadn't noticed before? How has your understanding of the novel changed as a result of this close reading?

References

Appignanesi, R., & Garratt, C. (1999). *Introducing postmodernism.* Cambridge, MA: Icon Books.

Applebee, A. N. (1993). *Literature in the secondary school: Studies of curriculum and instruction in the United States.* Urbana, IL: National Council of Teachers of English.

Appleman, D. (1993). Looking through critical lenses: Teaching literary theory to secondary students. In S. Straw & D. Bogdan (Eds.), *Constructive reading: Teaching beyond communication* (pp. 155–171). Portsmouth, NH: Boynton/Cook.

Atwell, N. (1998). *In the middle: New understandings about writing, reading, and learning* (2nd ed.). Portsmouth, NH: Boynton/Cook.

Baker, R. (1981). *Poor Russell's almanac.* New York: St. Martin's Press.

Barnet, S. (1996). *A short guide to writing about literature* (7th ed.). New York: HarperCollins.

Barthes, R. (1981). Theory of the text (I. McLeod, Trans.). In R. Young (Ed.), *Untying the text: A post-structuralist reader* (pp. 31–47). London: Routledge.

Beach, R. (1993). *A teacher's introduction to reader-response theories.* Urbana, IL: National Council of Teachers of English.

Bonnycastle, S. (1996). *In search of authority: An introductory guide to literary theory* (2nd ed.). Peterborough, Ontario: Broadview Press.

Boomer, G. (1988). *Metaphors and meaning: Essays on English teaching* (B. Green, Ed.). Densington & Norwood, Australia: Australian Association for the Teaching of English.

Brown, R. (1993). *Schools of thought: How the politics of literacy shape thinking in the classroom.* San Francisco: Jossey-Bass.

Cherland, M., & Greenlaw, J. (Eds.). (1998). Literary theory in the high school English classroom. *Theory into Practice, 37*(3), 175.

Cochran-Smith, M., & Lytle, S. L. (Eds.). (1993). *Inside/outside: Teacher research and knowledge.* New York: Teachers College Press.

Crews, F. C. (1965). *The Pooh perplex.* New York: Dutton.

Crowley, S. (1989). *A teacher's introduction to deconstruction.* Urbana, IL: National Council of Teachers of English.

Derrida, J. (1989). Structure, sign, and play in the discourse of the human sciences. In P. Rice & P. Waugh (Eds.), *Modern literary theory: A reader* (pp. 149–165). London: Edward Arnold.

Desai, L. (1997). Reflections on cultural diversity in literature and in the classroom. In T. Rogers & A. Soter (Eds.), *Reading across cultures: Teaching literature in a diverse society* (pp. 161–177). New York: Teachers College Press.

Eagleton, T. (1983). *Literary theory: An introduction.* Minneapolis: University of Minnesota Press.

Elkind, D. (1986). *All grown up and no place to go: Teenagers in crises.* Reading, MA: Addison-Wesley.

Emig, J. (1990). Our missing theory. In C. Moran & E. F. Penfield (Eds.), *Conversations: Contemporary critical theory and the teaching of literature* (pp. 87–96). Urbana, IL: National Council of Teachers of English.

Fecho, R. (1993). Reading as a teacher. In M. Cochran-Smith &. S. L. Lytle (Eds.), *Inside/outside: Teacher research and knowledge* (pp. 265–272). New York: Teachers College Press.

Fetterley, J. (1978). *The resisting reader: A feminist approach to American fiction.* Bloomington: Indiana University Press.

Forrester, V. (1980). What women's eyes see (I. de Courtivron, Trans.). In E. Marks & I. de Courtivron (Eds.), *New French feminisms* (pp. 181–182). Amherst, MA: University of Massachusetts Press.

Galda, L. (1983). Research in response to literature. *Journal of Research and Development in Education, 16*(3), 1–6.

Gates, H. L., Jr. (1992). *Loose canons: Notes on the culture wars.* New York and Oxford: Oxford University Press.

Graff, G. (1987). *Professing literature: An institutional history.* Chicago: University of Chicago Press.

Graff, G. (1991, April). Debate the canon in class. *Harper's,* pp. 31–35.

Graff, G. (1992). *Beyond the culture wars: How teaching the conflicts can revitalize American education.* New York: Norton.

Graff, G. (1995). Organizing the conflicts in the curriculum. In J. F. Slevin & A. Young (Eds.), *Critical theory and the teaching of literature: Politics, curriculum, pedagogy.* Urbana, IL: National Council of Teachers of English.

Greene, M. (1988). *The dialectic of freedom.* New York: Teachers College Press.

Greene, M. (1993). The passions of pluralism: Multiculturalism and the expanding community. In T. Perry & J. Fraser, *Freedom's plow* (pp. 185–196). New York: Routledge.

Griffith, P. (1987). *Literary theory and English teaching.* Philadelphia: Open University Press.

Grossman, P. (1990). *The making of a teacher: Teacher knowledge & teacher education.* New York: Teachers College Press.

Guerin, W. L., Labor, E. G., Morgan, L., & Willingham, J. R. (1992). *A handbook of critical approaches to literature* (2nd ed.). New York: Oxford University Press.

Guth, H., & Rico, G. (1996). *Discovering literature.* Upper Saddle River, NJ: Prentice-Hall.

Hillis Miller, J. (1989). Deconstruction and *Heart of darkness.* In R. C. Murfin (Ed.), *Heart of darkness: A case study in contemporary criticism.* New York: Bedford-St. Martins.

Hines, M. B. (1997). Multiplicity and difference in literary inquiry. In T. Rogers &

A. Soter (Eds.), *Reading across cultures: Teaching literature in a diverse society* (pp. 116–134). New York: Teachers College Press.

Hynds, S., & Appleman, D. (1997). Walking our talk: Between response and responsibility in the literature classroom. *English Education, 29*(4), 272–294.

Johnson, B. (1981). Translator's introduction. In J. Derrida, *Dissemination* (pp. xv–xvii). Chicago: University of Chicago Press.

Kolondy, A. (1985). Dancing through the minefield: Some observations on the theory, practice, and politics of a feminist literary criticism. In E. Showalter (Ed.), *The new feminist criticism: Essays on women, literature, and theory* (pp. 144–167). New York: Pantheon.

Leggo, C. (1998). Open(ing) texts: Deconstruction and responding to poetry. *Theory into Practice, 37*(3), 186–192.

Lynn, S. (1990). A passage into critical theory. In C. Moran & E. F. Penfield (Eds.), *Conversations: Contemporary critical theory and the teaching of literature* (pp. 99–113). Urbana, IL: National Council of Teachers of English.

Lynn, S. (1998). *Texts and contexts: Writing about literature with critical theory* (2nd ed.). New York: Longman.

Marshall, J. (1991). Writing and reasoning about literature. In R. Beach & S. Hynds (Eds.), *Developing discourse practices in adolescence and adulthood* (pp. 161–180). Norwood, NJ: ABLEX.

McCormick, K. (1995). Reading lessons and then some: Toward developing dialogues between critical theory and reading theory. In J. F. Slevin & A. Young (Eds.), *Critical theory and the teaching of literature: Politics, curriculum, pedagogy* (pp. 292–315). Urbana, IL: National Council of Teachers of English.

Meier, D. (1995). *The power of their ideas: Lessons for America from a small school in Harlem.* Boston: Beacon Press.

Moore, J. N. (1997). *Interpreting young adult literature: Literary theory in the secondary classroom.* Portsmouth, NH: Boynton/Cook

Moore, J. N. (1998). Street signs: Semiotics, *Romeo and Juliet,* and young adult literature. *Theory into Practice, 37*(3), 211–219.

Murfin, R. C. (Ed.). (1989). *Heart of darkness: A case study in contemporary criticism.* New York: Bedford-St. Martins.

Nelms, B. (Ed.). (1988). *Literature in the classroom: Readers, texts, and contexts.* Urbana, IL: National Council of Teachers of English.

Perkins, Gilman, C. (1973). The yellow wallpaper. Old Westbury, NY: Feminist Press. (Original work published 1892)

Perry, W. G. (1970). *Forms of intellectual and ethical development in the college years: A scheme.* New York: Holt, Rinehart & Winston.

Pirie, B. (1997). *Reshaping high school English.* Urbana, IL: National Council of Teachers of English.

Probst, R. (1988). *Response and analysis: Teaching literature in junior and senior high school.* Portsmouth, NH: Boynton/Cook.

Purves, A., Rogers, T., & Soter, A. O. (1990). *How porcupines make love: Notes on a response-centered curriculum* (2nd ed.). New York: Longman.

Rabinowitz, P. (1987). *Before reading: Narrative conventions and the politics of interpretation.* Ithaca, NY: Cornell University Press.

Rogers, T., & Soter, A. O. (Eds.). (1997). *Reading across cultures: Teaching literature in a diverse society.* New York: Teachers College Press.

Rose, M. (1995). *Possible Lives: The promise of public education in America.* Boston: Houghton Mifflin.

Rosenblatt, L. (1968). *Literature as exploration* (2nd ed.). Noble & Noble.

Sauer, B. (1995). Making connections: Theory, pedagogy and contact hours. In J. F. Slevin & A. Young (Eds.), *Critical theory and the teaching of literature: Politics, curriculum, pedagogy* (pp. 341–354). Urbana, IL: National Council of Teachers of English.

Scholes, R. (1985). *Textual power: Literary theory and the teaching of English.* New Haven, CT: Yale University Press.

Scieszka, J. (1999). *The true story of the 3 little pigs, by A. Wolf.* New York: Viking Kestrel.

Selden, R. (1989). *A reader's guide to contemporary literary theory.* Lexington, KY: University Press of Kentucky.

Shelley, M. (1992). *Frankenstein.* In J. M. Smith (Ed.), *Frankenstein: Complete, authoritative text with biographical and historical contexts, critical history, and essays from five contemporary critical perspectives.* Boston: Bedford Books of St. Martin's Press. (Original work published 1818)

Showalter, E. (Ed.). (1985). *The new feminist criticism: Essays on women, literature, and theory.* New York: Pantheon.

Showalter, E. (1989). Toward a feminist poetics. In R. Con Davis & R. Schliefer (Eds.), *Contemporary literary criticism* (pp. 457–478). New York: Longman.

Sizer, T. (1986). *Horace's compromise: The dilemma of the American high school.* Boston: Houghton Mifflin.

Slevin, J. F., & Young, A. (Eds.). (1995). *Critical theory and the teaching of literature: Politics, curriculum, pedagogy.* Urbana, IL: National Council of Teachers of English.

Smith, M., & Rabinowitz, P. (1998). *Authorizing readers: Resistance and respect in the teaching of literature.* New York: Teachers College Press.

Sontag, S. (1969). *Against interpretation, and other essays.* New York: Dell.

Thomson, J. (1993). Helping students control texts: Contemporary literary theory into classroom practice. In S. Straw & D. Bogdan (Eds.), *Constructive reading: Teaching beyond communication* (pp. 130–154). Portsmouth, NH: Boynton/ Cook.

Tyson, L. (1999). *Critical theory today: A user-friendly guide.* New York: Garland Press.

Willinsky, J. (1998). Teaching literature is teaching in theory. *Theory into Practice, 37*(3), 244–250.

Willis, A. (1997). Exploring multicultural literature as cultural production. In T. Rogers & A. O. Soter (Eds.), *Reading across cultures: Teaching literature in a diverse society* (pp. 116–132). New York: Teachers College Press

Wolf, D. P. (1988). *Reading reconsidered: Literature and literacy in high school.* New York: College Entrance Examination Board.

Selected Literary Texts

NOVELS AND PLAYS

Chopin, K. *The awakening.* New York: Simon & Schuster, 1899.

Conrad, J. *Heart of darkness.* Reprint, Peterborough, Ontario: Broadview Press, 1995.

Dreiser, T. *Sister Carrie.* Reprint, Philadelphia: University of Pennsylvania Press, 1981.

Fitzgerald, F. S. *The great Gatsby.* Reprint, New York: Scribner, 1953.

Glaspell, S. *A jury of her peers.* Boston: Small, Maynard, 1920.

Golding, W. *Lord of the flies.* New York: Aeonian Press, 1954.

Guest, J. *Ordinary people.* New York: Viking Press, 1976.

Guterson, D. *Snow falling on cedars.* New York: Vintage Books, 1994.

Hawthorne, N. *The scarlet letter.* Reprint, New York: Modern Library, 1962.

Huxley, A. *Brave new world.* Reprint, New York: Perennial Library, 1946.

Ibsen, H. *A doll's house.* Reprint, New York: S. French, 1972.

Kafka, F. *The trial.* Reprint, New York: Schöcken Books, 1998.

Katz, J. *Running fiercely toward a high thin sound.* Ithaca, NY: Firebrand Books, 1992.

Morrison, T. *Sula.* New York: Random House, 1993.

Morrison, T. *Beloved.* New York: New American Library, 1987.

OBrien, T. *The things they carried.* Boston: Houghton Mifflin, 1990.

Orwell, G. *Nineteen eighty-four.* San Diego: Harcourt, Brace, 1949.

Salinger, J. *Catcher in the rye.* Boston: Little, Brown, 1951.

Shakespeare, W. *Romeo and Juliet.* Reprint, Cambridge and New York: Cambridge University Press, 1955.

Shakespeare, W. *Hamlet, prince of Denmar*k. Reprint, Cambridge and New York: Cambridge University Press, 1985.

Shelley, M. *Frankenstein, or, the modern Prometheus.* Reprint, Berkeley: University of California Press, 1984.

Steinbeck, J. *Of mice and men.* Reprint, New York: Viking Press, 1965.

Updike, J. Separating. In *Problems and other stories.* New York: Knopf, 1979.

Wharton, E. *The age of innocence.* New York: Grosset & Dunlap, 1920.

Woolf, V. *A room of one's own.* New York: Harcourt, Brace, 1929.

Wright, R. *Native son.* New York and London: Harper & Brothers, 1940.

Wright, R. *Black boy: A record of childhood and youth.* New York: Harper & Row, 1945.

POETRY

Auden, W. H., "The unknown citizen"
Blake, W., "I saw a chapel"
Bly, R., "The executive's death"
Coleridge, S. T., "Kubla khan"
Donne, J., "Death be not proud"
Frost, R., "The road not taken"
Keats, J., "Bright star, would I were steadfast as thou art"
Naruda, P., "Ode to my socks"
Plath, S., "Mushrooms"
Roethke, T., "My papa's waltz"
Shakespeare, W., "Shall I compare thee to a summer's day?"
Shakespeare, W., "Sonnet 18"
Stafford, W., "Traveling through the dark"
Swenson, M., "The universe"
Thomas, D., "Do not go gentle into that good night"
Wordsworth, W., "I wandered lonely as a cloud"

Index

About the Author

DEBORAH APPLEMAN is the Class of 1944 Professor of Educational Studies and the Liberal Arts and director of the Summer Writing Program at Carleton College in Northfield, Minnesota. Professor Appleman earned her doctorate in 1986 from the University of Minnesota. A former president of the Minnesota Council of Teachers of English, she currently serves on the executive committee of the National Council of Teachers of English's Conference on English Education. She has been a member of NCTE's Standing Committee on Research and served as co-chair of NCTE's Assembly for Research as well as the special interest group in literature for the American Educational Research Association.

Professor Appleman was a high school English teacher for 9 years, working in both urban and suburban schools. She continues to work weekly in high schools with students and teachers. Professor Appleman's primary research interests include adolescent response to literature, multicultural literature, adolescent response to poetry, and the teaching of literary theory in high school. She is the author of many articles and book chapters, and, with an editorial board of classroom teachers, helped create the multicultural anthology *Braided Lives*.